Praise for *Yes, You Can Innovate*

'Pithy, practical and packed with compelling studies and useful tools. If innovation matters to you – and it should – read this book with a highlighter in hand!'

Scott Anthony, Managing Partner, Innosight; author, *The Little Black Book of Innovation* and *The First Mile*

'The 6 'I's of Innovation® is a simple yet powerful framework for planning, executing and delivering innovation in any organisation. Natalie's book is an essential companion on an innovator's bookshelf!'

Charlie Ang, Founding President, The Innovators Institute; Ambassador, SingularityU, Singapore

'A rarity – a practical approach to innovation. There are many academic texts on innovation but this is that rare phenomenon – a book that helps everyone to apply innovation principles every day. And, even better, it has been tried and tested in global institutions.'

Professor Steven Myint, Senior Fellow A*Star; Chairman of Innovations Exchange

'Natalie Turner is one of the leading innovation practitioners globally. This excellent book is packed with practical tools and examples to help those who want to innovate, profile their strengths, develop their skills and bring ideas to life. It will also help innovation leaders build the capability and impact of their teams.'

Roland Harwood, co-founder and Managing Director, 100%Open

'If innovation is key to your strategy, read *Yes, You Can Innovate*. It not only provides a single model for innovation management, but shows how important people are to be generating and making new ideas happen. It also gives practical ideas for how to engage them in the innovation process. An insightful read that will complement any organisation's programme for growth.'

Danny Wootton, Head of Innovation, ISS, Ministry of Defence

'Having worked with Natalie and the Six 'I's® for some years now, it is a joy to be able to refresh the various aspects of the Model through the book. It is easy to read, either from end-to-end or to dig into specific areas you want to explore in more detail. At the same time, it is a practical book as it deals with reality … rather than just focusing on theory … it is very much about what you can/should do and not about what others have done before you. One of the aspects that separates this book from others is the inclusion of an assessment tool which is very useful for putting together or evaluating current teams embarking on a journey of innovation through the six steps of the Model. If you deal with any kind of business development or innovation, this is a book that is worth reading and using.'

Michael Meyer, Director of People and Communications, LEO Pharma Asia

'*Yes, You Can Innovate* is an easy-to-read set of practical tools and tips which can be used to help you innovate, and, as a founder, leader and owner of an SME, it helps me to support my staff to value the importance of innovation. I highly recommend it if you want to start, or continue, your innovation journey.'

Gabriel Helmy, CEO and founder, The Capacity Specialists

'I have known Natalie Turner for many years and I have admired her no-nonsense approach to creativity and innovation. She knows where the gaps are and what tools and strategies are required to enable individuals and organisations to embark on a strong and successful Innovative journey. At last, here is a book that is truly practical and easy to follow and with ideas that are time-tested and wonderfully illustrated. Natalie's 6 'I's® are complemented by her 6 'C's™: together they make for REAL Innovation. A must read for all who want to know what innovation is and how it can be realised.'

Dr Kirpal Singh, author, *Thinking Hats and Coloured Turbans: Creativity Across Cultures;* Chief Academic Officer, Training Vision Institute

'Natalie Turner's extensive experience shines through in this empowering manual for anyone looking to create and embrace change. Start using it now to identify your own strengths for innovation, amplify these with the right mindset, and build stronger partnerships'.

Anna Simpson, author, *The Innovation-Friendly Organization* and *Chief Innovation Coach at Flux Compass*

'A very practical guide that will enable you and your organisation bring innovation to life. *Yes, You Can Innovate* is packed full of activities, tools, and resources that will help you to improve your innovation processes and culture.'

Christi Novomesky, Portolio and Launch Program Manager, Kellogg's Snacks APAC

'An essential primer for innovation success, with the tools to get your idea right, the necessary skills and behaviours for the journey, and the critical factors for creating an impact. Whether a start-up business or an established company, *Yes, You Can Innovate* will make your innovation succeed'.

Pamela Hamilton, author, *The Workshop Book;* Managing Director, Workshop Cookbook

'Innovation is a survival skill in today's disruptive world. Natalie's book dispels the myth that innovation is the purview of the exceptional among us and a fascinating read in putting structure to many things that I have known instinctively or acquired through experience. It is a life skill that can and should be learnt and cultivated. This book is the key to unlocking your inner innovator.'

Lavinia Thanapathy, President, PrimeTime Business and Professional Women's Association

'People in organisations are hungry for ways to become more innovative, whether it is in their product or service delivery, or in their ways of working. This is the practical guide that they, and the consultants that work with them, have been waiting for.'

Denise M. Morris Kipnis MSOD, founder and Principal, Change Flow Consulting

'Natalie Turner, whose journey I have observed with great interest and admiration for over a decade, has written a remarkable book which is offering a path through the jungle of innovating that is both easy to understand and practical in its application. One important aspect in which it differs from other innovation books is that it brings together the different stages of the innovation journey (process) with the different mindsets (people) that are required at each stage if we are to succeed. Structured around her Six 'I's® Model – which readers are invited to complete – the book is full of tips, tools and further reading. It should convince everyone that they can indeed contribute to innovation.'

Dr Bettina von Stamm, innovation philosopher, storyteller, catalyst, Innovation Leadership Forum; author, *Managing Innovation, Design and Creativity*

'*Yes, You Can Innovate* is a must-have book for every HR and OD professional, leader of teams and business coach, and for everyone who knows that innovation has long ceased to be the work of only a few. In today's day and age, being able to innovate is table-stakes for a successful organisation, a great career and for a fulfilled life. Natalie's book offers a wonderfully comprehensive and well-rounded framework of the stages of innovation and opens it to everyone. It's a guide and teacher; it inspires, gives great insight into needed competencies and the mindsets of innovation. And it doesn't end there ... it offers a multitude of ideas and activities for individuals and teams to embrace the mindsets to innovate and to strengthen their capabilities ... You will not only read this book once, it will be a great companion for a long time!'

Monika Steimle, Director of People Strategy,
SAPIENT RAZORFISH

YES, YOU CAN INNOVATE

Pearson

Natalie Turner

Yes, You Can Innovate

DISCOVER YOUR INNOVATION STRENGTHS AND DEVELOP YOUR CREATIVE POTENTIAL

Harlow, England • London • New York • Boston • San Francisco • Toronto • Sydney
Dubai • Singapore • Hong Kong • Tokyo • Seoul • Taipei • New Delhi
Cape Town • São Paulo • Mexico City • Madrid • Amsterdam • Munich • Paris • Milan

Pearson Education Limited
KAO Two
KAO Park
Harlow CM17 9NA
United Kingdom
Tel: +44 (0)1279 623623
Web: www.pearson.com/uk

First edition published 2018 (print and electronic)

ISBN: 978-1-292-21816-8 (print)
9781292218175 (PDF)
978-1-292-21818-2 (ePub)

British Library Cataloguing-in-Publication Data
A catalogue record for the print edition is available from the British Library

Library of Congress Cataloging-in-Publication Data
A catalog record for the print edition is available from the Library of Congress

Cover design by Two Associates
Cover images © Ayoub Moulakhnif

Print edition typeset in 9.5/13, Helvetica Neue LT W1G by iEnergizer Aptara®, Ltd.

NOTE THAT ANY PAGE CROSS REFERENCES REFER TO THE PRINT EDITION

20 2022

CONTENTS

ABOUT THE AUTHOR

Natalie Turner is an experienced innovation and leadership development specialist, voted by CMO Asia and the World Federation of Marketing and Sustainability as one of the top 50 female leaders in Asia. She has worked for and consulted with some of the world's leading organisations, including The Development Bank of Singapore (DBS), LEO Pharma Asia, Kellogg's, Singapore Airlines and Cisco Systems, helping them build innovation systems, culture and capabilities as well as generating new ideas to help them grow their teams and businesses. Natalie is also an international speaker on innovation, entrepreneurship and leadership and an experienced business facilitator, trainer and consultant.

Natalie is the inventor of The Six 'I's of Innovation®, an integrated methodology and assessment tool that helps individuals and organisations measure their innovation strengths. It is also a clear step-by-step guide to make innovation more practical and effective. She has three degrees; a BA Hons in Politics & Legislative studies, an MSc in Economics and Social Psychology and an MBA. From London, Natalie is now based in Singapore and works across Asia and internationally.

www.6-i-innovation.com
www.yesyoucaninnovate.com

AUTHOR'S ACKNOWLEDGEMENTS

'You know so much about this – you should create your own innovation model,' said Neil, a good friend and mentor of mine. We sat in a London coffee shop discussing next steps for the innovation consultancy I had created. It was 2009 and the recession was biting hard. 'You have been working in this field long enough, have tons of experience and organisations need something that is simple, yet practical, to help them innovate.' Neil was right. I had identified a gap in the market for a more person-centred approach to creating and developing ideas. It was a challenge to which I was ready to rise.

Little did I know that, eight years later, I would have moved to Asia, established a business in Singapore and be writing a book, which codifies over 20 years of research and innovation experience into a practical how-to guide – The Six 'I's of Innovation®.

There are many people who have been part of my journey whom I would like to acknowledge. Too many to name all. Here are a few that deserve a special mention. Pamela Hamilton, who introduced me to the world of using customer insights as a springboard for new ideas; Kim Barnes and Dr David Francis for their excellent programme Managing Innovation; Neil Metha, my business mentor, who encouraged me to be an inventor and introduced us to United Kingdom Trade and Industry (UKTI) who helped us set up in Singapore; Michael Gold, a close friend and colleague who worked with me to develop the initial concepts and prototype them into the real world; Dr Gilles Spony, award-winning cross-cultural psychologist, for his research rigour and investigative skills in testing the statistical reliability of the Model; clinical psychologist, Lilian Ing, for her help and advice on the IP development and her ongoing support since I arrived in Singapore; Dr Kirpal Singh, whose speaking invitation to Singapore Management University (SMU) brought me to Asia in the first place; and David Forrest, who saw my *PURPOSE* before I did.

Our supportive clients, a few to whom I would like to give special acknowledgement – Danny Wootton, Pauline Pinnock, Jan Crabtree, Rick Teo, Francisca Ghin, Lynn See, Michael Meyer, Marco Brabec, Michael Maigret, Monika Steimle, Christi Novomesky, Deanna Sacco, Rose Shapley and Pat Lucas – for applying The Six 'I's® on real business innovation challenges to create value for yourselves and your organisations.

My colleagues: my fellow director in Singapore – Shoba Chandran, who continues to grow not only our business, through our Certification Programmes and partnership network, but is furthering the ideas into experiential tools and products; Andy Bruce who has developed, with his innovative App software, a Six 'I's® online innovation management system; Ayoub and Mohd, our two Upwork designers whom we have never met; Rob and Stu for creating our Six 'I's® profile management system and my editor Eloise Cook who, with her practical insight and advice, has helped ground my thinking to make this book more useful and practical.

No first book would be complete without thanking those that are closest to me. Those who have seen and shared the highs and lows of this innovation journey – my sister, Caroline Slark, who, with her generous assistance, enabled us to move to Asia; my supportive parents Leslie and Jean Turner, who brought me up to be an innovator and, despite being in their eighties, continue to remain curious explorers willing to challenge themselves courageously and enthuse others; and my husband and co-founder Carl Hinds, who has been my business partner since 2006. His financial and operational role, combined with his commitment, love and patience, has made the journey of The Six 'I's® possible. He is my greatest believer and supporter.

Natalie Turner
Singapore, January 2018

PUBLISHER'S ACKNOWLEDGEMENTS

We are grateful to the following for permission to reproduce copyright material:

Exhibit on page 93 from https://www.inc.com/paul-schoemaker/brilliant-failures/why-failure-is-the-foundation-of-innovation.html; interview on page 48 from Rick Teo Interview on page 77 from Marco Brabec; interview on page 106 from Jacquie Ford; interview on pages 134–136 from Thomas Nyegaard; interview on pages 165–166 from Christine Sim; interview on page 194 from Rose Shapley.

We would like to thank Ayoub Moulakhnif for designing the cover image, icons, logos and the figures appearing within this book.

FOREWORD

YES, YOU CAN INNOVATE

Innovation matters – of course. If we do not change what we offer the world (our products and services) and how we create and deliver them (our processes) there is a good chance we will not be around very long. There is plenty of evidence to link innovation with business survival and growth and it is the same in the world of social innovation – we need to think hard about how we can create value from ideas.

In English, 'innovation' is an interesting word, since we use it both as a noun and as a verb – 'to innovate'. In its noun form, we are interested in the outcomes – the things that change, whether they are new products or services, business models or process improvements. But innovation is also a 'doing word' – and, if we are serious about innovation, then we need to think hard about how we make change happen.

It is not easy – not least because these days we are living in a version of 'Red Queen world'. The famous character in *Alice in Wonderland* reminds us, in a great scene, of the challenge of change. After she and Alice have been running for what seems like ages, Alice stops and, panting, tells the Queen, '… in our world you'd get somewhere else if you'd been running very fast for a long time, as we've been doing!' To which the Red Queen imperiously replies, in a condescending tone, 'A slow sort of country. Now here, you see, it takes all the running you can do to stay in the same place. If you want to get somewhere else you must run at least twice as fast as that!'

That is a powerful metaphor for today's environment. Whether we are concerned with business or social change, the challenge is the same – how to innovate? And this is trickier than it looks. It is not enough just to recognise the importance, to say how much we believe in innovation. If we are serious about it, then we have to acknowledge that it is not like the cartoons. That well-known picture of a lightbulb flashing above someone's head is a great starting point, a good idea – but there is a lot more to innovation before we can create value from the idea.

The good news is that we know a lot about this process. Studies of how we organise and manage innovation date back at least a century and there have been thousands of studies – different countries, sectors, firms, different methods, different data sets. They all point towards the same core principles, lessons learned the hard way form experience about what we should and should not do to stack the innovation deck in our favour.

This is a rich resource on which we can draw – but it also raises another question. There is plenty written about innovation, but the vast majority of it is couched in terms of what 'the organisation' should look like or do. How we should structure, the different kinds of policies and procedures we should follow, the ways we interact in an increasingly fluid 'open innovation' world. Far less writing covers the world of the individual, what he or she can do and the skills they might need to effect change.

There is, of course, a category dealing with 'entrepreneurs', but much of this is about heroes – supermen and women who defeat the odds, take risks and deliver value in their startups. But this literature neglects the many other individuals – 'quiet entrepreneurs' – who act as change agents inside organisations or in their communities. They may never turn out to be tech. billionaires, but what they are doing is, recognisably, innovation. Indeed, as the eminent management writer Peter Drucker neatly put it, 'innovation is what entrepreneurs do' – and they can do it in all sorts of contexts.

So, this book is welcome because it focuses fairly and squarely on the individual and the kind of skills they need to be effective agents of change. Innovators are not born – innovation is a skill set that can be learned and practised. (Indeed, studies of 'serial entrepreneurs' often underline the learning process they have gone through in acquiring what now seems to be their magic touch.) So, it makes sense to try and distil these lessons and make them available in a structured format.

Even if it is a long and winding road, there is a structure to the journey of innovation – and this book offers a helpful roadmap. It draws on a great deal of personal experience, but also dips into the relevant research underpinnings of the field. Importantly, it is filled with practical tools and activities to help flesh out the skill sets involved and how they can be practised and developed. In fact, it does not seem to be the kind of book that is designed to be consumed passively – there are too many points along the way where you are invited to reflect and to act.

At its heart is a simple framework, The Six 'I's® – and these explain the ways in which an individual can make sense of the innovation challenge and develop the key skills to enable it to happen. Importantly, a key assumption in the book is that people have different strengths in their profile as innovators – it is not a case of one size fits all. Understanding your particular type can help you play to your strengths, but also recognises where and how you might benefit from adding others to your team or network with complementary profiles.

These days we do not have to look too far to see how important the innovation agenda has become – the word is everywhere. But, too often, this is simple sloganeering, espousing the importance of the idea without providing any linkage to how it could be made to happen. Just saying 'we believe in innovation' does not get us very far. If we are serious about making the journey, then this book offers not only an excellent starting point for anyone committed to this path, but also plenty of useful help and guidance to keep you going along the way.

PROFESSOR JOHN BESSANT

Professor John Bessant is currently the Chair in Innovation and Entrepreneurship at the University of Exeter and has visiting appointments at the universities of Erlangen-Nuremburg and Queensland University of Technology. In 2003, he was elected a Fellow of the British Academy of Management and, in 2016, a Fellow of the International Society for Professional Innovation Management (ISPIM). He has acted as advisor to various national governments and international bodies, including the United Nations, World Bank and OECD. He is the author of 30 books, including, in collaboration with Dr Joe Tidd, the seminal text *Managing Innovation: Integrating Technological, Market and Organisational Change*.

TO BEGIN

INTRODUCTION

We know we are living in a time of exponential change, hyper competition and globalisation. In fact, futurists say what we are experiencing now is just the tip of the iceberg. The world will change so dramatically over the next 30 years that what we see as breakthrough innovation today will pale into insignificance tomorrow. The most important human survival skill will be our ability to consistently create value out of new ideas.

Being prepared for this change is critical to our continued existence. Our world desperately needs new thinking, new ideas and new solutions to some of the most complex problems that human beings have ever faced. To be an innovator is to be a pioneer of bringing the new into the world, but it is not just about being creative. It requires a complex and diverse raft of skills and ways of thinking. It also requires the application of new thinking to everyday situations – what I call day-to-day innovation. All of us, whether we are pioneering breakthrough technologies or working in an operations department of a logistics company, can make a difference. More importantly, all of us have a reason for being – a *Purpose*, a contribution to make – with our lives, our talents and our skills.

Yes, You Can Innovate is a practical book that will help you to understand what innovation is, why it is important and how to create ideas and make them happen.

It will:

- Outline a clear six-stage process on how to innovate
- Help you to understand and develop your individual strengths
- Build skills to compensate for your challenges and know how to partner with others
- Provide tools, tips and strategies for developing your innovation skills and mindsets

Structured around a proven methodology: *Yes, You Can Innovate* incorporates The Six 'I's of Innovation®, an integrated framework to help improve your ability to create value out of new ideas. Used by individuals and corporations around the world, including Cisco Systems, Singapore Airlines and LEO Pharma Asia, The Six 'I's® is a simple system that covers six distinct stages – the journey of an idea, from its creative inception through to implementation and improvement:

1 **Identify** opportunities (to understand trends and potential areas of growth)
2 **Ignite** ideas (to create novel solutions)
3 **Investigate** (to prototype, test and research ideas)
4 **Invest** (to have courage and persuade others to back ideas)
5 **Implement** (to make an idea happen and create value from it)
6 **Improve** (to optimise, scale and learn from success and failure)

All stages are interlinked by an overarching *Purpose* or intent, to help you think through what you want to create and the problem you want to solve.

While the business buzzwords of our time will change – human skill, mindset and behaviour will still need to be applied. We will still need to *identify* opportunities, *ignite* ideas, *investigate* whether they will work, *invest* in them, *implement* the idea into the world and *improve* on what we have done.

Below are key terms, and a simple explanation, for the definitions that I use in the book.

CORE DEFINITIONS

- **Innovation** – the ability to create value from ideas that are new to a person or organisation
- **Skill** – the ability coming from one's knowledge, practice and aptitude to do something well
- **Behaviour** – a range of visible actions made by people towards their environment
- **Mindset** – a set of attitudes that shape thinking about oneself and the world

Imagine an iceberg. Below the water line is our mindset. Above the water line are our observable skills and behaviours – or how we choose to use our mindset and show up in the world around us.

EXAMPLE: RIDING A BICYCLE

Skills required to ride a bicycle are usage of the pedals and coordination.

Behaviours required to ride a bicycle are concentration and balance.

Mindset required while riding a bicycle is determination and persistence.

When you look at a child riding a bicycle for the first time, you can observe their behaviours as they try to master using the pedals and coordination (skills). They are not normally very aware of their environment and do not have the ability to adapt to change, often falling off as they learn, despite their concentration and attempts at balance (behaviours). As they improve, they start to become more aware of their surroundings, of people or potholes in the road or cars passing by. Through determination (mindset), their skills and behaviours become second nature and they start to feel confident, becoming more aware of their context (behaviour) and open and responsive to change. It is these elements – skills, behaviours and mindsets – working together, that help us to do things effectively. In addition to having a novel and workable idea, our ability to innovate – to create value out of new ideas – requires the conscious fusion of the three.

UNDERSTANDING THE SIX 'I's® MODEL

I am going to take you on a journey that I hope will help you develop and improve the three elements outlined in the Introduction and inspire and challenge you to stretch your thinking about how you can contribute to bringing new ideas into the world.

Any journey requires guidance to help navigate the unknown terrain. The Six 'I's of Innovation® is the guide that I have created to help simplify what often is seen as a complex, chaotic and unpredictable process.

On the inside cover of the book you will see the image of The Six 'I's® with an overview of the six core stages.

Below are six points to help you interpret the Model.

1 *The Six 'I's® is a circular Model*. This is because innovating does not follow a clear linear process. It has dead ends, roadblocks and unforeseen challenges. You will need to go backwards and forwards, across The Six 'I's® before you create something that is considered valuable.

2 At the centre of the Model is *Purpose* (or intent). This serves as an anchor point and, if applied more rigorously in how we think and how we work, would help to ensure that what we are trying to create will have *Purposeful value*. Here, we can objectively question and revisit what we are trying to do and question why. Here, we can, and must, move backwards and forwards to the other stages of the Model. From *investigate* back to *identify* or *ignite*, for example.

3 There are two coloured triangles, the same colour as their corresponding 'I' that link each of the stages with *Purpose*. These represent *process* and *culture*:

   - Innovation *process.* Each phase of innovation requires processes to support its effectiveness. For example, a process for capturing ideas at the *ignite* phase.
   - Innovation *culture.* As well as processes, each phase of innovation requires distinct cultural and environmental capabilities to reinforce certain types of behaviour. Often teams or organisations will fail because they have too much of one type of culture, for example, strong at encouraging new ideas in the *ignite* phase, but weak on building a culture that is skilled at *implementation*.

4 Although, from a teaching standpoint, we start with *identify*, in the real world your role in innovation may start at any of the stages of the Model. *It is not always the same starting point.* There are also many examples – ideas that are *ignited* and have no identified opportunity, for example.

5 *It mirrors the way that we think.* Although some of us may have a tendency to jump a stage, we do not stay neatly in one area; our mind moves backwards and forwards generating ideas, selecting them, improving on ideas and moving them forward into implementation and back again.

6 The Model can be a guide for *managing innovation projects* that we are working on by helping us to be more conscious of how we are working and where we are at any one point in the innovation journey. It can also be dialled up or dialled down – for thinking innovatively in our day-to-day work, as well as managing a more complex innovation project.

Each of The Six 'I's® requires different skills, capabilities and supporting processes that need to be maximised if you, your team or organisation are to innovate consistently and effectively. Each 'I' is also linked to a particular attitude or a mindset that is distinctive to that phase of innovation.

Innovation stage	**Mindset**
Identify	Curiosity
Ignite	Creativity
Investigate	Critical
Invest	Courage
Implement	Commitment
Improve	Clever

For example, when you are in the *investigate* phase, you need to be more *critical* about your ideas than when you are in the *ignite* phase, where a *creative* mindset is of paramount importance. If you are too critical in the *ignite* phase, you will kill off any new ideas before they have time to take root and grow.

On the inside cover, you will see a visual representation of each of these core orientations or mindsets – the primary attitude that is required within that stage of innovation.

DISCOVER YOUR INNOVATION STRENGTHS – HOW TO TAKE THE SIX 'I's® ASSESSMENT

As part of the purchase of this book, you can discover your innovation strengths by completing The Six 'I's® assessment online. It will take you about 10 minutes to complete.

The questionnaire assesses your skills profile, around the six distinct stages of innovation. As a self-assessment tool, it is only indicative of your strengths, as perceived by you. Your results are not absolute and cannot be interpreted as competences or true abilities.

In order to improve innovation skills, it is useful to understand the perception of your current strengths. Use your results to increase self-awareness, build on your strengths and create dynamic teams and organisations that can innovate effectively and productively.

Once you have completed the questionnaire, you will receive a Report. Inside the Report is a graph that gives you an overview of your innovation strengths.

This will show your scores on each 'I'. You will see that you are not just one 'I', but a combination, some stronger than others. This is what we call your unique innovation style.

The graph overleaf shows someone whose core innovation strength is *identify*. You will see, however, that he has varying scores on the other five 'I's, with *investigate* as his lowest score. He is likely to be good at *identifying* opportunities and *igniting* ideas, also, to a degree, looking at how to *improve* on existing ideas. He may well miss the *investigate* stage altogether, jumping straight into *invest* and *implement*, but these are not his core strengths either. These areas are his potential blind spots and areas he will need to compensate through either developing skills or collaborating with those who have these areas as strengths. Within a team environment he will be a good strategic thinker and idea generator, but less interested in making the idea work. This is where he will need to partner with other people who are stronger in those skills so that he can improve his likelihood of success.

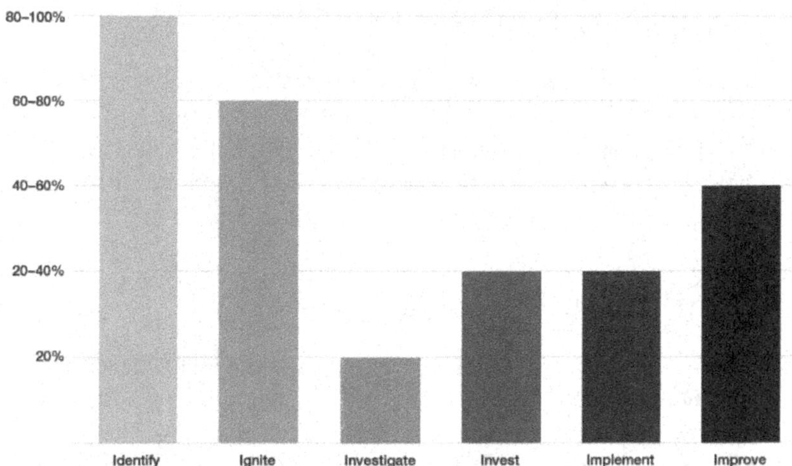

The Six 'I's® results – innovation strengths profile

The overall score is not an average of his results, it is normed against a database of other people who have completed the questionnaire who also deem themselves strong, or not so strong, on the different 'I's.

Within this book, there is a description of each 'I'. This includes strengths and challenges as well as the role each 'I' plays within the innovation process and the type of mindset that is required. Actively use this information, alongside your report, as you work through the book.

As you are a mix of 'I's, take that into consideration when you read your report as the various mix of 'I's will have an impact on how you innovate. For example, if you are high on *ignite* and *implement*, but low on *investigate*, you may well perceive your strengths as someone who is strong at generating new ideas and jump straight into action. It may well serve you to learn how to appreciate the *investigate stage*, by either developing some of the *investigator* skills in your own skill set and/or teaming up with other people who are strong in this area of innovation.

It is also useful for you to know your lower scoring 'I's so you make sure that you are developing skills that are important to your work. If you do not compensate for the areas in which you are not strong, and they are important to you, you are in danger, from a skills perspective, of not being able to innovate successfully. Seek out those around you who have these as strengths, as they can help accelerate your ability to do something well. Increasing your self-awareness will help you realise the importance of other skills to generate new ideas and make them work.

WORKING WITH DIFFERENT STYLES

As you learn to enhance your strengths and build new skills, invariably you will be working with people who are different from you. Take into account how the different styles on The Six 'I's® like to be communicated with. This will help you see from their perspective and build better team relationships.

STATISTICAL RELIABILITY

As people have a very different way of scoring themselves on a questionnaire – for example, some use a full scale, others do not, some have a tendency to score high on all questions, others low – the raw scores have been standardised. This takes away bias and helps to make the assessment more robust and meaningful. The standardised results have also been normed within a global population of people that have completed the questionnaire. This will give you a sense of not only what you think about your strengths, but also how you compare to a broader sample of people who also consider themselves strong or not on each of the 'I's.

Please keep your proof of purchase and visit our website www.yesyoucaninnovate.com. On the site, you will see details about how you can access the questionnaire.

HOW THE BOOK IS STRUCTURED

I have designed and structured this book to be like a manual, a how-to guide about practical innovation skills.

There are six main parts, structured around the core themes of each of The Six 'I's®:

- Identify
- Ignite
- Investigate
- Invest
- Implement
- Improve

Introduced with a story, and the strengths and challenges of the profile of that particular 'I', each chapter then focuses on three core elements:

- The skills
- The mindset
- The resource guide

Each chapter covers the skills, mindset and resources to help you understand and improve your ability to get better at that stage of innovation. There are also lots of examples and illustrations that I hope will help to bring innovation to life.

SKILLS

First, I cover six discrete skills that are important to the stage of innovation being explored. Of course, the skills can be useful in other stages of the innovation journey, but in that particular phase they carry more weight and importance. After a description and example of each, I will introduce you to a range of core *activities* and *tools*. Some of the tools are well-known and publicly available through other sources, some are proprietary. It is not intended as an exhaustive guide, but a digest that I have selected to help you generate opportunities and ideas and increase the likelihood of success. Where you are interested, you can use the Resource Guide at the end of each chapter to delve deeper. For ease of reading, the activities and tools are summarised in a table at the beginning of each chapter.

I also outline some tips on how to communicate with people who have strengths in the 'I' under discussion as well as some warning signs that may happen if you miss this particular stage of innovation.

MINDSET

Second, I cover the relevant mindset associated with the 'I'. Like the skills, the mindset is useful in other stages, but in that particular stage it is the orientation that most needs to be cultivated. For example, at the *ignite* stage, *creativity* is absolutely fundamental if we are to generate new solutions to the challenges or problems we are trying to solve.

I also include a range of 'Try This' Tips to help you develop the associated mindset of that chapter.

At the end of the Mindset overview, there is an interview with an individual who has used The Six 'I's® in their organisation, with examples of how they have used their profile and how it has helped them to be more successful at innovating.

RESOURCES

Third, I outline resources that you can refer to if you want to build up your knowledge on that particular 'I'. This includes articles, books, websites and other ideas that you might find useful. You can come back to the Resource Guide at any time.

Activities	
Tools	
Resources	
Try This	

HOW TO GET THE MOST OUT OF THIS BOOK

Real application will help you to improve your innovation skills, learn about how to apply your strengths and reveal where you may need support to improve your likelihood of success. So, if you have:

1 an innovation challenge
2 a new business idea
3 a new project in mind
4 or just want to get better at improving your skills

. . . this book can help you get organised. Buy yourself a notebook where you can collect your thoughts and ideas as you progress through the chapters and actively work through and apply the activities and tools, alongside the results from your Six 'I's® assessment, to help you reinforce the skills and mindsets.

There are three ways that you can approach this:

1 If you prefer to get a sense of the whole journey before you embark on the first step, read the chapter that outlines your top strength first and then read the book from cover to cover to get a sense of where your strength fits within The Six 'I's® skill set. Then, start again, working your way through some of the activities.
2 If you like to work methodically through a process, read the book as a step-by-step guide to help you think through each stage and how it can apply to your work.
3 You can also use the book on team innovation projects and work through some of the activities and tools in each chapter with other people.

By the end of reading this book, you will be able to:

- Understand a clear process on how to innovate (The Six 'I's® of Innovation).
- Understand your innovation strengths and challenges (The Six 'I's® assessment).
- Know a range of skills that will help you (The Six 'I's® skill sets).

- Experience using tools to improve your innovation skills (Six 'I's® tools and activities).

It is my *Purpose* that you are inspired to develop your skills and talents and contribute to new solutions that will create impactful and lasting value in the world.

So, let us begin.

PURPOSE

IT IS A QUESTION OF PURPOSE

Running through the centre of The Six 'I's® Model, is *Purpose*, which leads us to think through the 'why?' of innovation.

What does *Purpose* mean? Very simply, *Purpose is the reason for why something is created or for which something exists*. *Purpose* is very powerful, as it acts as an anchor to the whole of the innovation journey, a place that we can return to where we can think through what we are doing and why.

There are two types of *Purpose*: personal and collective. When the two come together, there is a stronger sense of synergy and alignment. We all know what it feels like to be off *Purpose*, doing work that does not fulfil us or line up with our values. Sometimes, for a variety of reasons, we have to do work we do not find particularly motivating, but, if we are able to discover our inner *Purpose* – what drives and motivates us – and find, or create, work or projects that fulfil this internal drive, then this will help to keep us going on the road of innovation when the going gets tough. And it will.

Purpose is also different from having goals. Goals are things we want to achieve in the future, that we are working towards. They are out in front of us. There is nothing wrong with goals, we need them. They help us to focus our energy and give us a destination of where we want to be, but they can also leave us in a sense of anticipation and unfulfilled desire, particularly if they are not linked to an inner *Purpose*. A word that I use interchangeably with the word *Purpose* is *intent* and, from intent we derive the word *intention* or how our attitude shapes the outcome of our action and behaviour.

As author Mark Matousek says, 'Intention is different (from goals) because it exists in the present moment and is based on presence, not planning … it is about connecting with our essential *Purpose* that leads us toward well-being rather than conflict. Intention keeps us aligned with our own core values.'

While this is not a book on discovering your personal *Purpose*, it is important that you think about what you value and what is important to you in relation to what you are trying to do with regards to innovating. Finding personal *Purpose* takes work. Just as much as then defining what it is you really want to do with your time and how you want to contribute your skills and talents to something that is bigger than what you could do alone. It is also far more enjoyable to feel like you are doing work that gives you a sense of internal satisfaction and impact.

Then there is collective *Purpose* or what we do in collaboration with others. The work that we conduct. The projects that we get involved in, the businesses that we start. Throughout the book, I refer to cases and stories of people who have innovated, big and small, known and unknown. What you will find, with most of them, is a sense of personal and collective purpose coming together. For example, in the chapter on *implement*, I share the story of Anita Roddick, the founder of the Body Shop. Her personal purpose was deeply held values about the environment and cosmetic industry and an intention to create an alternative to what was available for consumers. Her collective Purpose led her to create an organisation that could become a vehicle for this, which later grew to become a global business.

Think through the Purpose of what you would like to do. When you start a new innovation project, take some time to reflect on this before you begin. This will help to clarify your thinking and, if you are collaborating or working in a team with others, create shared understanding and alignment of what each of you expects. It will also help you to define the parameters for *identifying* where opportunities might be emerging for doing something new.

Innovation is about the creation of value. It is about generating an impact or an outcome. Within organisations, financial value is often the first thing that comes to mind and it is, of course, very, very important. However, when you are defining your Purpose, think more broadly than just financial impact. Think deeply about what you are trying to achieve and the type of value you want to create.

Below are some types of value you can think about when you start to define your Purpose.

- **Financial value:** the monetary, material or assessed worth of an asset, good or service.
- **Competitive/strategic value:** a superiority gained by an organisation when it can provide the same value as its competitors but at a lower price, or can charge higher prices by providing greater value through differentiation.
- **Social value:** refers to wider financial and non-financial impacts that goods and services might create, including the well-being of individuals, communities and social capital creation.
- **Environmental value:** refers to benefits derived from engaging in practices that have a positive impact on the natural environment.
- **Personal value:** refers to value derived at the personal level.

Are there other types of value that are important to you?

As well as being at the centre of the Model, Purpose is central to each stage of the innovation journey. It is, perhaps, the most important element as it is a place that you can revisit to evaluate what you are doing and why.

The first exercise I encourage you to do is to create what I call a Purpose Statement.

WHAT IS A PURPOSE STATEMENT?

A Purpose Statement is a short, succinct sentence that will help to give you clarity about what it is you want to do and why. It should use simple language that can be understood by someone who knows nothing about your area of expertise.

A good statement should help you to make decisions and keep you on track as you embark on your innovation journey. For example, if you have six ideas to choose from at the *ignite* phase and they are all strong, examine them in light of your *Purpose Statement*. Which one will help you achieve your intention or which one has closest alignment to what you want to do? The others might be good ideas, but not the best ones for you to *investigate*. Which ideas are also closest to your personal Purpose or in conflict with it?

TOOLS

Create a Purpose Statement

Use the statements here to help you think through what you are doing and why. This will help you to be clear on your *Purpose* from the start.

If you are working in, or managing, a team, use the questions to invite participation and exploration. This will help to create alignment about what you want to achieve together.

First, answer these questions:

1 I/We need to do this because …

2 I/We want to do this because …

3 My/our customers/stakeholders will benefit because they will receive/be able to …

4 I/We will benefit because …

5 This is in line with my personal Purpose because …

6 My/our *Purpose* is to …

Once you have answered the questions above, write a statement that clarifies what you are trying to do.

Your final statement should be crisp and concise.

For example, for *Purpose* of The Six 'I's®, answers to the questions are:

1 **I/We need to do this because …** innovating is often difficult and unpredictable and people don't know where to start or how to do it.

2 **I/We want to do this because …** it will highlight the importance of skills in creating and implementing new ideas and give a simple and straightforward process on how to generate ideas and bring them to life.

3 **My/our customers/stakeholders will benefit because they will receive/be able to …** know their strengths and the strengths of their team members and have a practical process, with supporting tools and methodologies, that they can apply and reuse. This will help to improve their likelihood of success.

4 **I/We will benefit because …** we will have a scalable Model that will create value across industries and geographies.

5 **This is in line with my personal Purpose because …** I am personally passionate about learning and creativity and inspiring and enabling others to create ideas and bring them to life.

The Six 'I's® Purpose Statement reads as follows:

The Six 'I's® Purpose Statement

To build a learning and assessment tool and methodology supported by products, services and processes that will enable individuals and organisations to create ideas and bring them to life.

Revisit the questions, and your Purpose Statement, as you progress through this book, particularly in the *ignite* and *investigate* phases.

Are the ideas that you are generating helping you to achieve what you want to do?

Use the following questions to help you reflect on what you are trying to achieve and to get great clarity on your overall intention.

Purpose reflection

Ask yourself the following questions:

- Has your *Purpose* changed? If so, what has it changed to? Be clear on this.
- Will the ideas you have generated fulfil the *Purpose* of what you want to do?
- Are the ideas that you have created in alignment with your personal values and motivations?
- If you are working with other people, are you all in agreement? If not, work to get clarity on what it is you want to achieve.

THE PURPOSE RESOURCE GUIDE

BOOKS THAT HELP TO EXPLORE PURPOSE

Kurtzman, J. (2010) *Common Purpose: How Great Leaders Get Organizations to Achieve the Extraordinary*. John Wiley & Sons.

Mourkogiannis, N. (2008) *Purpose: The Starting Point of Great Companies*. St Martin's Griffin.

Reiman, J. (2013) *The Story of Purpose: The Path to Creating a Brighter Brand, a Greater Company and a Lasting Legacy*.

Sinek, S. (2011) *Start with Why: How Great Leaders Inspire Everyone to Take Action*. Penguin.

Sinek, S. (2017) *Find Your Why: A Practical Guide for Discovering Purpose for You and Your Team*. Portfolio Penguin.

DISCOVERING YOUR PERSONAL PURPOSE

Holden, R. (2013) *Authentic Success: Essential Lessons and Practices from the World's Leading Coaching Programme on Success Intelligence.* Hay House UK.

Matousek, M. (2017) *Writing to Awaken: A Journey of Truth, Transformation & Self-Discovery*. New Harbinger.

Robinson, K. (2010) *The Element: How Finding your Passion Changes Everything*. Penguin.

Strecher, V.J. (2016) *Life on Purpose: How Living for What Matters Most Changes Everything*. HarperOne.

Warren, R. (2004) *What on Earth Am I Here For? The Purpose Driven Life*. Zondervan.

IDENTIFY

UNDERSTAND TRENDS AND POTENTIAL OPPORTUNITIES FOR GROWTH

'So, Natalie, what you are saying is that you don't think we should be investing any more money in this business?' said a senior leader, a slight smirk on his face. It was the late 1990s and the pre-paid mobile phone was just starting to gain momentum. I was in my late twenties and a junior strategic analyst, in my first proper corporate job. Who was I to say what the future held? I could feel the heat rise in my face as I told my senior managers what I thought. The market was changing fast and we needed to look beyond our phone card competitors to pre-paid mobile offerings and voice-over internet protocol (VoIP), both of which were still emerging as disruptive technologies. What was I expecting, a positive response?

Due to a changing regulatory environment, the business models underpinning telecommunications were being reinvented. It was a time of great discontinuity – the convergence of information technology, telecommunications and content – and the way people interacted online, although only early days, was starting to merge.

My role was to spend time networking, going to conferences, discovering new trends both social and technological, that the department should be aware of so that we could adapt our products and services to a changing environment. It was growing rapidly; new people were being hired and there was a lot of enthusiasm and activity. The leadership was investing multi millions into the development of a new card technology platform that allowed customers to make calls by copying numbers from their phone card into their landline phones or payphones.

Looking out over the horizon I could identify lots of opportunities for the company across the landscape of telecommunications and mobile technology, which I largely believed were being ignored by senior leadership.

Leaving the meeting, I was concerned. I walked back to my desk and looked at my computer screen. Why couldn't they see it? Why did they hire me to scout for new opportunities only to not listen to what I had to say? I sat there for a few minutes wondering what to do, and then I thought, 'Well, if they can't see it, I can, I need to get out of here!'

I started to browse the corporate intranet for jobs in other parts of the company and, after a while, I found one that looked interesting, in a small and obscure department that focused on internet technology. I thought, 'Now, here is the future.' I applied for a role heading up competitor intelligence and strategy and, after being interviewed, got the role and moved jobs. Within months, quicker than I had anticipated, there was a mass exodus of staff leaving the card department as it started to contract. The millions that had been spent on a technology platform became redundant, as competitors, both internally and within the broader market, made card services, and its nearby pay phone department, largely obsolete.

This story can be replicated many times over, in different industries, and at different times, as new technologies start to disrupt the status quo. In countless organisations there is an underlying belief that the competitive dynamics of the industry in which they operate are stable and that competitors are very similar entities following the same rules. This is just not the case anymore. A current example is the explosion of organisations such as Uber and Airbnb who have broken the rules of competition in transportation and accommodation. Both own no tangible assets – fleets of cars or hotels – and have transformed their respective industries.

My story was from the late 1990s. Discontinuities and disruption are happening at a faster pace now, so we need to be individually ready to *identify* what is going on, whether we are working inside an organisation or for ourselves. Like a submarine under the surface of the sea, we need to keep our eyes and ears open to the weak signals that are emerging and be ready to act.

I have told this story to illustrate the importance of our ability to be open and *curious* so we can *identify* opportunities, the subject for this chapter. *Identify* is about the ability to notice where gaps are arising that could give opportunities for ideas that could result in new products, services, processes, business models or ways of working.

The *identify* skill set is about being future-orientated and having the ability to spot areas that could be fertile for change. It is about being able to visualise the future – such as understanding emerging technologies that could cause industry disruption or being able to make sense of social attitudes and trends that are changing the buying behaviour of customers.

From a leadership perspective, it is the strength and confidence to focus direction so that you know where to place your effort and energy on areas that have strategic importance.

From the data that we have gathered across the world, the *identify* skill set is uniformly weak across many types of organisations and individuals. Why? Largely because being good at *identification* means deviating from day-to-day business activity and short-term results orientation. It means thinking differently, more expansively and, ultimately, if there is to be action, changing direction. This is often very hard to do.

Identifiers, those who have high confidence in this area, are often misunderstood in organisations. They can see ahead, sometimes too far, so others do not take them seriously. Or, at best, others find them interesting but not relevant to what needs to be done today. If organisations are to be serious about developing entrepreneurial talent, then encouraging *identifiers* and creating a culture that encourages these skills needs to be seriously nurtured and developed.

THE IDENTIFIER PROFILE

Innovation role – Providing vision, direction and a sense of new possibilities
Mindset – Curiosity

Identifier's strengths:

1 Visualising and imagining the future.
2 Making sense of trends and patterns and thinking about what they might mean for opening fresh opportunities.
3 Being forward thinking, strategic and noticing and seeing things that other people don't.
4 Being curious and having lots of different interests and a huge appetite for learning.
5 Having a positive outlook on life and seeing opportunities where others see problems.
6 Outward looking and interested in the world around them.
7 They often seek to add new people, whom they believe will bring new thinking, to their networks.

The swirling image illustrates the mindset of ***Curiosity****. It is open-ended, dynamic, explorative and able to generate momentum.*

Identifier's challenges

As with all strengths, particularly if they are overdone, there can be challenges.

- As identifiers are usually big-picture thinkers, they can often miss the detail.
- As they are future-orientated, they can lose focus on the present day.
- They can get easily bored if not stimulated by new things, new ideas and new ways of thinking.
- If intellectually driven, they can sometimes be too abstract or conceptual in how they explain things to other people.

If they are good at leading others, *identifiers* enjoy providing strategic focus to their teams and organisations. They are also good at fostering a culture and environment that helps others to seek new areas of opportunity, inspiring people with their grand plans and big-picture thinking.

Within an organisational context, *identifiers* need to learn how to influence others around them as they can often be the initiators of new ways of seeing and thinking, which organisations desperately need if they are to innovate. If they do not manage to do this, they often end up frustrated, despondent and misunderstood.

The challenge for *identifiers* is to learn how to communicate in ways that people will understand as well as to inspire others about possibilities for the future.

HOW TO COMMUNICATE WITH *IDENTIFIERS*

Depending on the mix of 'I's on someone's profile, here are a few do's and don'ts that will help you communicate more effectively with *identifiers*.

Do's	Don'ts
Stay open-minded to possibilities and opportunities	Narrow down areas of discovery too quickly or just focus on the present
Give them time to explore emerging trends that are orientated towards the future	Involve them in work that is focused on maintaining current systems and processes
Stimulate their imagination with grand visions and big plans	Limit their sphere of work to the ordinary
Encourage them to pioneer and trail blaze the unknown	Restrain their thinking to only solving day-to-day problems and challenges

THE IDENTIFY SKILLS

While there are many skills that help us to identify opportunities, we will focus on six core attributes critical to this stage of innovation:

1 To envision and imagine the future
2 To see and understand trends
3 To have a positive outlook and spot opportunities
4 To expand personal connections and networks
5 To enable others to look for new opportunities
6 To provide strategic direction for others to explore possibilities

Let us look at each one in turn.

Throughout the chapters, I give examples and stories to help illustrate, and bring to life, this stage of innovation. I also include practical ways, or activities and tools, to help you improve your ability and confidence to *identify* opportunities. Here is a top-line summary of the skills and their associated activities and tools.

Skills	**Tools**	**Activities**
To envision and imagine the future		Increase exploration skills (mental, physical and social)
To see and understand trends	Trend analysis, PESTLE	
To have a positive outlook and spot opportunities	Customer persona Insight generation	Develop your skills of observation
To expand personal connections and networks		Expand your networks
To enable others to look for new opportunities		Create space for fresh thinking
To provide strategic direction for others to explore possibilities	Prioritisation of opportunity areas	

SKILL ONE – Being able to envision and imagine the future

The world is dynamic and evolving. One place that affects most of you reading this book is the workplace. While a lot of people are still expected to get up and go to a building and sit in front of a computer for 8 to 10 hours a day, interspersed with meetings and other activities, how we work is changing. Traditionally, businesses have relied on a series of middlemen (or intermediaries) to get work done. For example, in the past, if you wanted to build a new website, you would have to go to an agency in your own country that designed websites.

Nowadays, many of those organisations are being removed from the traditional supply chain and new intermediaries are being formed. One such intermediary is Upwork. We use Upwork, mostly for graphic and design support, but Upwork covers all manner of different services. Our team is largely made up of people we have never met, never interviewed and some we have never even spoken to. They come from diverse backgrounds and countries such as Morocco, India and Malaysia. We collaborate using the Upwork platform and they produce some of the highest-quality work we have ever purchased. They are productive, efficient, creative and responsive. They deliver results and we pay them. As they do not have the overheads of expensive offices and all the trimmings associated with agencies, they can keep their costs low. They are also living in economies where the US Dollar, the currency they are paid in, can go a long way, making them incredibly competitive to anyone offering the same service from countries such as the UK, the USA or Singapore. When we see online market places emerging such as this, what does it tell us about how work is evolving and what may happen to existing models of management in the future?

To be good at visualising the future we need to develop our exploration skills. With online search tools, we are not short of access to knowledge. You can explore worlds you have never been to – whether they be physical countries, industries, topics or themes. I can remember the world before the internet, and it was not that long ago. I can also remember going to libraries and using encyclopaedias and reference books to do research. No need for that any more. Make time for exploration.

ACTIVITY

Increase your exploration skills

- **Mental exploration:**
  - Read widely.
  - Listen to interesting people that expand your mind, for example speeches that are published through virtual or traditional media on a subject that you know nothing about.
  - Learn about trends that are shaping the world.
- **Physical exploration:**
  - Explore different parts of your country, places you have never been to before, for example if you are a 'city' person, take a weekend to explore the countryside and see what nature can teach you.
  - If physical travel is financially restrictive, then engage in metaphorical travel. For example, browse through travel sites.
  - Eat food you have never tried before.
  - Learn a new skill or hobby.
- **Social exploration:**
  - Spend time talking to people who are older than you, younger than you or people who like different things outside your areas of interest. See what you can learn.
  - Look at what other people or organisations are doing, particularly those that are seen to be on the fringes or edges of new discoveries.

SKILL TWO — Being able to see and understand trends

It is one thing to see the future; it is another thing to make sense of it. Identifiers are good at sense making. They can see what is happening, not as random events, but as interconnected threads that weave together to make a pattern.

For example, over the next few years, how we provide services to older people will change dramatically. What are the big trends that are affecting this industry? Regulatory and political changes are one, but there are many others: the advancement and accessibility of tele-health services and technological changes; the growth of proactive wellness; the upward trend of people living longer; the attitudes of baby boomers towards institutional living and getting older; the rise in dementia and other brain-related diseases, and many others. In researching trends, small spaces start to emerge; openings that, to the curious mind, could give rise for innovation.

Identifiers keep an open and broad mind to the big influences that are affecting their work or industry. Things are changing. What trends are affecting the area you want to innovate within?

TOOLS

Trend analysis

1 What has shaped the area you want to innovate within in the past?
2 What is shaping it now and how fast is it changing?
3 What are the big changes that are coming on the horizon, even if they seem unlikely now, that could shift how things operate today?
4 Make a list of the trends that are affecting the area in which you want to innovate.
5 What impact will each trend have on your project idea or challenge?

Trend one ______________________________

Impact ______________________________

Trend two ______________________________

Impact ______________________________

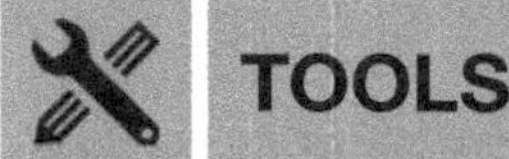

Pestle

One simple tool that is useful to get a bird's eye view of the big picture is PESTLE (**P**olitical, **E**conomic, **S**ocial, **T**echnological, **L**egal and **E**nvironmental). It is a good place to start to unpack the bigger trends that are affecting the area within which you are interested in innovating.

1 Use the example table as a guide and list down all the things that are affecting you, in each of these areas (or others if not on the list here).

2 What insights do you gain from this exercise? Do any patterns start to emerge?

Political	**Economic**	**Social**	**Technological**	**Legal**	**Environmental**
Type of Government	Taxes	Population Growth	Emerging Technologies	Consumer Laws	Climate
Government Stability	Economic Growth	Educational Systems	Rate of Technological Change	Employment Laws	Geography
Trade Restrictions	Interest Rates	Employment Rate	Research and Development Activity	Health and Safety Laws	Propensity for Natural Disasters
Press Freedom	Exchange Rates	Age Distribution	Degree of Automation	Industry Regulations	Weather
Corruption	Economic Changes	Attitudes Towards Work	Speed in which Automation is Displacing Jobs	Antitrust Laws	Legal
Employment Legislation	Foreign Investment	Social Mobility	Degree of Technological Disruption	Discrimination Laws	Corporate Social Responsibility

SKILL THREE — Being able to have a positive outlook and spot new opportunities

Back in the early 2000s, I had the privilege of working in an innovation bureau at a large international research firm. Here I was exposed to several innovation methodologies that helped companies understand the needs of their market, whether consumers or business users. One of these was called Insight Generation – the ability to be able to understand what the needs of people are and the frustrations that they face in trying to fulfil these needs.

Insights are generated through observing people and the problems that they face. Think of a simple example: flat beds in an aeroplane. A simple insight would be: 'I need to arrive at my destination refreshed and ready for work, but I feel cramped and can't sleep because I am so uncomfortable.' An insight immediately gives rise to ideas and solutions to meeting these needs, such as Virgin Atlantic's J2000 angled lie-flat seat in 1999.

Often, we equate the ability to innovate with the ability just to be creative, which we will cover in the *ignite* section of this book but, really, we need something before that. We need to be able to *identify* needs so we can see where opportunities might emerge. Before the flat bed, business travellers just put up with feeling cramped, as there was no alternative available. It was a problem. The ability to *identify* opportunities looks below the surface of a problem to uncover the deeper need or frustration that it is being revealed. There lies the opportunity for new ideas and solutions.

Getting better at seeing opportunities starts with increased observational skills.

Customer persona development

It is easy to say innovation needs to be centred on customers, but who is your customer? A tool that will help bring your customer to life is what we call a *customer persona*, which represents the essence of a segment of people for whom you want to innovate. This includes, but goes beyond, demographical information, such as age, gender, income level, to more psychographic understanding, such as motivations, values and interests.

1 Use the following headings to think through who your customer is:

Demographics

- Age range
- Gender

- Income level
- Educational level
- Ethnicity
- Citizenship

Psychographics

- Attitudes
- Values
- Lifestyle
- Personality
- Interests

Find a picture to represent your *customer persona*.

2 What insight does this give you about who you need to observe, talk to and how to *identify* their needs?

ACTIVITY

Become an observer

1 Think about where you want to innovate: what is the problem you are trying to solve?

2 What are the needs and frustrations that surround the problem?

Immerse yourself in the problem through observing people and researching the area where you want to innovate and capture your observations into sentences:

- Use objective language: 'The man said …', 'I saw …', 'I noticed …', 'The report said …'.
- Write up your observations.

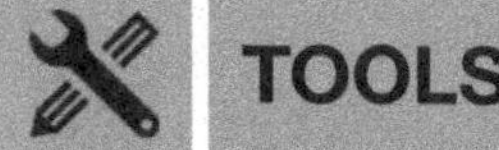

Insight generation

1 List all the needs that relate to the observations that may stop the problem being solved.
2 Write them into sentences using the words *need* and *but* in the sentence to spark creative tension.
3 Test your insights with potential customers.
4 Rank them. Which is the strongest?

For example, this simple insight gave rise to suitcases on wheels.

Observation: 'I saw that the man was struggling to lift his bag …'

Insight: 'The man *needed* to carry his bag *but* it was heavy and hurt his shoulder.'

This is what we call an *insight statement*.

DID YOU KNOW?

In 1970, Bernard Sadow, then vice-president at a luggage company in the USA, had a eureka moment as he carried two heavy suitcases through an airport while returning from a family holiday. As he waited at customs, he observed a worker effortlessly rolling a heavy machine on a wheeled cart. When he got back to work, he took casters off a wardrobe trunk and mounted them on a big travel suitcase. It worked. He patented the new product, taking note of his observations about how people, due to the growth in long-distance air travel and the decline in train journeys, were handling luggage in a new way. The patent stated, 'Whereas, formerly, luggage would be handled by porters and be loaded or unloaded at points convenient to the street, the large terminals of today, particularly air terminals, have increased the difficulty of baggage-handling.'

Although a great idea, he had trouble selling his rolling suitcase. It was a novel concept and people take time to adapt to a new way of doing something, even though it was better than what they had. People were used to either carrying their luggage or using small, fold-up wheeled carts to which they strapped suitcases and pulled behind them. They were slow to change.

He showed it to different department stores across New York City, and other potential retailers, and people just thought he was crazy. Finally, Macy's ordered some, and the market grew quickly, as Macy's ads began promoting 'the luggage that glides'.

Today's standard issue black suitcase, pulled on two wheels with a retractable handle, was invented nearly 20 years later in 1987 by Northwest Airlines pilot Bob Plath, who affixed two wheels and a long handle to suitcases that rolled upright, rather than being towed flat like Sadow's four-wheeled models. Plath initially sold his Rollaboards to fellow flight crew members. But when travellers in airports saw flight attendants walking through the airports with their Rollaboards in tow, a whole new market was created.

The flat bed and rolling luggage may not be innovations that changed the world, but they certainly are innovations that have made travelling a lot easier and more enjoyable.

They are also simple examples that illustrate the importance of observation and how being observant can help us to *identify* insights that can generate new opportunities for new products, services, processes and business models. Identifying opportunities does not always have to be about radical technological advances; small, often inconsequential, things can give rise to new opportunities for innovation.

We can read this example now and it seems so obvious, so ordinary, but how long did it take for human beings to create a solution to such a simple need? It is all a matter of observing, taking note and thinking laterally to *ignite* new solutions, the subject of the next part of the book.

SKILL FOUR – Being able to expand your connections and networks

One of the things I love about living in Asia is the diversity of people that I meet. It is not uncommon to go out to a social or business networking event and meet people of seven or eight nationalities. All from different industries and backgrounds. I also live in a multicultural neighbourhood surrounded by different festivals, foods, religions and ways of thinking. I find it easy to make new connections and enjoy the stimulus of talking to people. I am curious about their stories and their lives.

When we think of having large networks these days, often we think of how many friends we may have on different social media platforms, but this is not necessarily the type of network that I am talking about. It is not just how many 'friends' we have, or people that are linked in to us in some way that is useful, but the diversity of the connections and the quality of how we engage and interact with them, both on and offline.

The quality does not have to lead to a deep and meaningful friendship, although some connections do lead to that, but to enriching engagements that are useful for either or both parties. Why is networking such a critical skill for innovation? It is because it opens our minds to other perspectives and other ways of seeing. It can also accelerate our ability to do something faster when we can find people who can help us with the opportunity or problem that we want to explore or solve. It is about having an expansive and open mind to learning new things.

ACTIVITY

Expand your networks

Think about the people you are connected to. How diverse are they? So often, our circles of contacts, the people we engage with, are very small. Our contacts tend to be quite homogenous as we tend to be attracted to people like us. If we are surrounded by homogeneity, we will not create expansive ways of seeing. Here are some ideas to try.

1. Write down contacts in the area where you want to innovate that could help you accelerate your knowledge.
2. Who, in your network, do you know who can make introductions to fresh connections?
3. What networking events, conferences and online groups operate in the area in which you are interested? Join one and see what new connections you could make.
4. Aim to meet two new people a week.

SKILL FIVE – Being able to provide strategic direction for others to explore opportunities

It is one thing to develop these ways of thinking and seeing, but can you develop the abilities to help others do the same? Here we are talking about the ability to lead others to innovate, to help them to explore new areas of opportunity. This is where you start to amplify and leverage your own abilities so that you can extend your impact and influence. The days of the lone ranger innovating on their own are long gone. The world we live in is interconnected and global. Whether you are working independently or in a team, we are in relationships with others, sometimes across time zones, with people from all over the world. Our ability to inspire and encourage others to expand their thinking and see new opportunities is a great gift as it provides leadership. It also helps to create a conducive culture that can support innovation.

When I was a client director in a market research organisation, I encouraged the team to get together once a week and bring in articles, blogs, excerpts from books or videos that they found interesting about the broader context of the industries we were working within. I called these gatherings Freshness Spaces. It was a time for fresh thinking. The purpose was to open our minds, expand our horizons and help us see the trends that were affecting our clients' worlds. This gave us lots of stimulus for new ideas. It also helped us serve our clients better as we could bring fresh thinking to our conversations.

ACTIVITY

Creating space for fresh thinking

1 Find an opportunity where you could provide leadership and help to challenge other people's ways of thinking.

2 If you have a team, or are working with peers, put aside an hour where you can share ideas and information about the area in which you want to innovate rather than normal day-to-day business activities.

3 Create a regular Freshness Space to encourage yourself and others to learn new things and make fresh connections about your or their work.

Put it in your calendar and colour it in yellow so it stands out. Do not be tempted to remove it when your work becomes too busy.

It does not matter if you are working as an entrepreneur or in a large organisation. The important thing is to create the space for this to happen.

SKILL SIX – Being able to provide strategic focus so that opportunities can be identified

While you want to have an open mind that can visualise the future, make sense of trends and patterns, be curious and encourage others to do the same, you also need to channel and focus your attention. If not, your energy can disperse into multiple directions and end up being interesting but not very impactful. Often, I see this in more entrepreneurial organisations, both ones in which I have worked and ones that I have supported as a consultant. For example, all the leaders of one entrepreneurial organisation I worked with were high on *identify* and *ignite*. The company was full of ideas and had a sense of possibility and opportunity, but they could not focus. This led to frustration amongst employees who needed clear direction and, ultimately, they wasted their time and resources on pursing too many new projects. Lots of enthusiasm. Lots of excitement. Lots of ideas, but not much impact. To lead innovation, whether in yourself, or with a group of people, choices need to be made. This leads to focus.

We can liken an opportunity space as a playing field for one to explore. It has a perimeter fence that surrounds it with gaps in the slats of wood so we can see through to the other side. It does not constrict us, but gives us enough focus so we know where we should start our exploration for the emergence of new ideas.

TOOLS

Opportunity prioritisation

Revisit your *Purpose*. Look at the opportunity areas you have identified as potential spaces for innovation.

- Which ones best address your Purpose Statement?

- Rank them in order of importance.
- Select the opportunity area or insight that you think best fits your Purpose. It does not mean that you will not come back to the other opportunities and insights that you think are important. You might find that there is synergy between them or that they merge completely as you progress along the innovation journey. You, or your team, only have so much time and energy, so make sure that it has a clear focus before moving on to the *ignite* stage.

Opportunity area Name/title	Low fit to Purpose	Medium fit to Purpose	Best fit to Purpose
Opportunity 1			
Opportunity 2			

Innovating is not a linear process and it is possible that you could start your innovation project at any of the 'I's but, from a teaching perspective, we start with *Purpose* and *identify*, as it helps to give clear direction on where to go next and why. If a project or activity is given to you to work on by someone else, then ask yourself questions that are pertinent to the *identify* stage. This will help you think bigger about what it is you are trying to do.

Dangers of Missing Out the *IDENTIFY* Stage

- You (or your team) cannot agree on a suitable opportunity, so lack alignment and direction.
- You generate ideas but do not know what to do with them.
- You end up focusing on solving present problems and miss out on bigger opportunities.
- Your ideas may not solve a problem or unmet customer or market need.

THE IDENTIFY MINDSET

'A COMPELLING DESIRE TO LEARN OR EXPERIENCE SOMETHING NEW'

CURIOSITY

Rummaging around an old bookstore in London, I came across a bright yellow covered book, with one word on the front, 'Curious'. The book, written by Dr Todd Kashdan, uses science, story and practical exercises to show you how to become a curious explorer, what he terms 'a person who is comfortable with risk and challenge and who functions optimally in an unstable, unpredictable world'. It is a must read.

If you are to develop a mindset of curiosity, which, I believe, is closely linked to creativity, then you need to feed your mind with different sources of stimulus. I love to read novels and practise creative writing, for you it may be another activity. Perhaps it is something that you enjoyed when you were a young child or a hobby that you would like to spend more time on. It could be playing a musical instrument, dancing, acting, painting, playing a sport – whatever makes you feel like you are lost in another world. A world where there are no demands on your attention. I am not talking about the pressure of playing an instrument to pass exams, for example, but the love of playing an instrument just because you can, because it takes you to a place where there are no constraints.

There is something here about creating the space for this to happen. We know that many ideas are random, they come from nowhere it seems, and do not just appear in a brainstorming session at work. We are often under so much pressure to perform, to get things done, to make things happen, that we are chasing ourselves throughout the day, the week, the month, with rarely a second glance back at how we were doing all those things. The pace at which we were working, the frantic, meeting-orientated culture we are part of crams space out of our lives.

Being curious is also about not judging or labelling something too quickly or putting it in the 'I don't like box' or 'I'm not interested, it's not my thing.' We can develop a mindset of curiosity by not just discovering the new, but also by becoming reinterested in things and people that are familiar, to try and see with a new perspective.

If you are a parent or work with children, think about how you are nurturing curiosity. Luckily, I had parents who were non-conventional and who followed their own passions which, at the time, may have seemed detrimental to my educational development and at odds with the norms of society. Thankfully, it was the opposite. This is not just about fitting in the art class on a Tuesday night after school, but how you feed and nurture their young and open imaginations to be curious about the world around them and keep it alive, despite the often conforming nature of school.

For example, a friend has created a way for her family to learn about different countries by discussing the country's customs, dress, language and culture. They try out new recipes and eat together, practising different words and phrases from the relevant language. When I was a child, every Thursday, my parents, sister and I had a reading evening where we would pick a novel and read aloud to each other around the table after dinner.

Look around you. Notice how many couples and families go out and spend the whole time on their mobile phones. No discussion, no conversation, no social interaction. I know I have to stop myself reaching into my bag to scroll through social media sites, read emails or see if anyone has sent me a message. OK, we live in a connected world, but the compulsion is addictive and can be detrimental to the development of our curious, social selves.

In my speeches, I often talk about inserting the pause button, taking a deep breath, just stopping and watching, both yourself and others around you. This is not just good for being more present in life, it will also help your ability to think, to have new insights, as space is somehow, magically it seems, created and insights have room to percolate and bubble up to the surface. A curious mind is often a creative mind.

This brings us to the second 'I' of The Six 'I's of Innovation® which we will explore in the next chapter – *ignite*.

Want to Develop a Curious Mindset?

An orientation and attitude that has a fierce desire to explore, ask questions and to know more?

TRY THIS

1 Resurrect an old hobby or an interest that you once loved to do as a child and rediscover it. Dedicate an evening or part of a weekend to exploring this interest and notice how it makes you think and feel and if it stimulates your curiosity.

2 Pick an activity that you find unappealing or that you do not particularly enjoy, i.e. watching a sport you do not like, going to see a play that you think will be boring, listening to music that you do not normally listen to. Search for three things in the activity that you found unique or novel. Carry this open-mindedness throughout the week and see what else you notice.

3 Next time you reach for your mobile phone (out of habit), pause and stop yourself. Time how long you can go without looking at it and stay present to the conversation or activity that you are part of. What is happening around you?

4 Increase your observation skills: sit down on a bench for 10 minutes and just watch people as they pass you by. What do they look like? How are they acting? What does this tell you about human behaviour?

5 When in conversation with other people, try to remain open to whatever transpires, without making assumptions or categorising them or the topics you are discussing. Resist the temptation to judge.

6 When you are out this weekend, do not rush around. Slow yourself down and notice how you feel in your body. What sights do you see, what do you smell or hear?
7 Find someone who is interested in something you have no interest in. Ask them questions; find two things that are novel about what they are saying.
8 Try points 5, 6 and 7 for five minutes each and then increase them by 1 minute at a time, in different situations and with different people. Is more curiosity starting to emerge?
9 Practise, practise, practise.

Make these *curiosity* mindset activities part of your life.

READY TO MOVE ON TO *IGNITE*?

Use this simple checklist to make sure you have covered some of the most salient points of *identify*.

Activity	Complete
I have researched trends that are affecting my industry and feel like I have spotted an opportunity for innovation.	
I have thoroughly researched the area in which I want to innovate and observed real needs of customers through developing a customer persona (ideal customer).	
I have identified opportunity areas and have developed a clear customer insight which has a creative tension that needs to be solved.	
I have tried an activity that I have never tried before and feel my mind has expanded. I am actively building curiosity as a mindset in my daily life.	

To dig deeper into developing the skill and mindset refer to the resources at the end of this chapter, but first let us meet Rick Teo, whose highest score on The Six 'I's® is *identify*.

LET'S MEET RICKY TEO

THE IDENTIFIER PROFILE

Name:	Rick Teo
Job:	Senior area director, South Asia (Singapore)
Company:	LEO Pharma
Highest Six 'I's® rating:	Identifier

What challenge are you looking to solve with innovation right now?

Innovation is tough within the pharmaceutical market as it a highly regulated industry. There are a lot of things that we cannot do. This means that we need to innovate more, as many ideas will not be workable. Our headquarters is in Denmark, where our products are discovered, so innovation for us is in how we localise our portfolio of products across 13 countries within South Asia.

Looking at your Six 'I's® results, you're an *identifier*. How does this knowledge impact or change the way you work?

Due to the nature of the industry, and the slow pace in which it operates, the general mindset of people is often focused on what cannot be done, rather than on what can be done. But disruption is happening all around us, and our industry is changing too. My results impact the way I think about my role, and the importance of anticipating the trends that are shaping our environment. I need to support the business, be ready for change. This will prepare us for the next evolution of our growth.

How do you play to your strengths? What advice would you give other people who want to get better at *identify*?

Get out and about, talk to more people, as well as your peers, and spend time understanding insights – in our case, patient insights and the insights of health care professionals. You can't see what you can't see, so you need to see from other people's perspectives so you can *identify* gaps. Being good at *identify* doesn't always mean you identify the right things. So, you need courage. You need to be able to try. Not trying is tantamount to failure. Knowing my strengths has helped me reflect on how I work and also the importance of drawing on the diverse capabilities of team members.

What steps, if any, would you take to improve the areas where you are not so strong, or that are important to you and how?

The key area of focus for me is *investigate*. Some ideas are not good ideas after all, and there are others that I think won't work, that could, if they were investigated more thoroughly. I don't want to kill an idea, or approve of it straight away, but learn how to build this *investigate* bridge between an idea and its investment and implementation. One way is by bringing in subject matter experts on the areas that need deeper *investigation*. This will help to accelerate my learning and to help me see my blind spots. Another way is to continue having 'market dives' or planned excursions and thorough investigations of whether an idea might work in a particular country's market.

How has The Six 'I's® helped you and your teams/business? What examples, if any, can you share?

In partnership with HR, we conducted a Talent Development Programme across South Asia with a focus on innovation. We actively used The Six 'I's® as a framework and process for developing new commercial sales and marketing ideas, and how we could engage our Health Care Professionals (HCPs) to build closer relationships. One innovation that came out of this process was the development and roll out of a quality care digital platform and online applications to help HCPs support patients who have psoriasis.

Have you produced something you would consider innovative?

Back in 2013, we had 1 per cent market share in the Philippines with our product Fucidin®, an antibiotic preparation that helps people with skin infections. Despite having a licence to sell directly to patients via pharmacies – over the counter (OTC) – we had been promoting via the ethical/doctors channel, but it wasn't working. The market was flat for the last 10 years and we were seeing very minimal growth. We questioned our own mindset towards what we were doing and *identified* an opportunity to try something new. We *ignited* an idea to switch an integrated OTC promotional model, innovative for us, as it was a first in LEO Pharma Asia. We *investigated* different ways of promoting the product and made the *investment* to enhance product visibility as well as free skin screenings through partnership with drug stores and dermatologists. This helped us to increase our brand visibility and patient engagement. We *implemented* a marketing campaign through cable, national television, radio advertising and celebrity endorsement, which resulted, despite the competitive nature of the industry, in a growth of market share from 1 to 15 per cent. We continue to seek ways to *improve* what we have done both on this project as well as other 'cross-pollination' opportunities across South Asia.

THE IDENTIFY RESOURCE GUIDE

This chapter outlines some resources for further exploration to get better at identifying opportunities and developing the mindset of curiosity.

RESOURCE GUIDE

What your personal interests are will largely determine areas that you would like to research or know more about, but here are a few resources and techniques I use to open my thinking and seeing. What is important with these early stages of innovation is that you go broad, as well as deep. This will help your brain to make lateral connections between different things, which is often where the source of ideas springs from.

Here are some things to help you:

- Read the magazines *Fast Company* and *Wired* **www.fastcompany.com** and **www.wired.com**. Sign up for their newsletters, too; they are full of great ideas and stories of new things that are emerging.
- Can't go out and *be a trend-spotter* yourself? Use Springwise **www.springwise.com** – the world's largest idea-spotting network – to navigate the emerging world of new opportunities and ideas.
- **How to People Watch** – you can find a great guide on how and where to start on wikiHow: **www.wikihow.com/Begin-People-Watching**. Improving your skills as an observer is critical in being able to identify opportunities for innovation. This is where the curious mindset comes in -- to be like an anthropologist seeing and observing what is happening around you.

- Want to rub shoulders with others who are thinking big about the future? Join the World Future Society **www.wfs.org**. It is a community of individuals and organisations connected across the globe using a futurist mindset to tackle the world's biggest challenges.
- Every year, I commit some time and money to learning something new. I have joined raw food cooking courses in Bali, learnt about emerging psychologies in Australia, attended a novel-writing retreat in the temples of Angkor Wat in Cambodia, to name a few. On my list is to attend The Singularity University, an organisation with a 'mission to educate, inspire and empower leaders to apply exponential technologies to address humanity's grand challenges'. Can't attend in person? They have a range of resources on their website to inspire you (https://singularityu.org).

FURTHER READING

A few good books for thinking strategically

Anthony, S., Johnson, M. and Gilbert, C. (2017) *Dual Transformation: How to Reposition Today's Business While Creating the Future*. Harvard Business Review Press.

Chan Kim, W. and Maubourne, R. (2015) *Blue Ocean Strategy: How to Create Uncontested Market Space and Make the Competition Irrelevant.* Harvard Business Review Press.

Christensen, C. (2016) *The Innovator's Dilemma: When New Technologies Cause Great Firms to Fail*. Harvard Business Review Press.

Dyer, J., Gregerson, H. and Christensen, C. (2011) *The Innovators DNA: Mastering the Five Skills of Disruptive Innovators*. Harvard Business Review Press.

Lafley, A.G. and Martin, R.L. (2013) *Playing to Win: How Strategy Really Works*. Harvard Business Review Press.

Great books for stimulating curiosity

Cameron, J. (2002) *The Artist's Way: A Spiritual Path to Higher Creativity*. Jeremy P. Tarcher.

Kashdan, T. (2010) *Curious?: Discover the Missing Ingredient to a Fulfilling Life.* Harper Paperbacks.

IGNITE

CREATE IDEAS AND NOVEL SOLUTIONS

'So how many of you think you are creative?' I asked a large group of middle and senior managers. Two people put up their hands.

'So, what about the rest of you, do none of you consider yourself remotely creative?'

Maybe one or two more people slowly put up their hands.

Often, we ask this question when we facilitate innovation workshops or conduct speeches about creative thinking and, regardless of country or industry, the response is normally the same. Very few people in the world of corporate business, unless they are in the creative industries, think that they are creative.

'So, having completed a few activities to generate new ideas, how many of you now consider yourself just a little bit more creative than you did at the beginning of this workshop?' I asked, as we reflected on the morning's learnings. Three quarters of the group puts up their hands.

Why is this the case?

Despite the rallying cry for more creative thinking to solve the complex challenges we face today, the ability to originate, generate and create new ideas is often a skill that many individuals and organisations find hard to cultivate.

The fact of the matter is that our brains are far more pliable than we have been led to believe. With the growing awareness of neuroplasticity – literally, the ability of the brain to change itself – we can, in fact, transform our minds, even if it takes a lot of effort. By the end of our time together, participants are not only relieved, but also surprised, when they realise that, given the right tools, stimulus and environment, they can create some unique and novel ideas.

But being trained in creative thinking or attending workshops can only go so far in developing our creativity. Developing a creative mindset takes a lot of effort: not only are we having to do things we may have never done before, which can feel strange and unfamiliar, we are, literally, rewiring the way we think.

The importance of the ability to be creative, to *ignite* new ideas is the subject of this chapter.

The *Ignite* phase is central to innovation. This includes generating lots of new ideas, continually seeking new knowledge outside your current areas of interest and challenging your way of thinking. Looking for connections between different and unrelated ideas is also important, as this is often where the spark for innovation happens.

It is not always about being original, but being able to combine often different ways of thinking to create something new. Think of the wheel and the bag talked about in the *Identify* chapter. Creating a culture where people feel free to contribute their ideas and motivate others is an important leadership skill as these are factors that help to create a trusting environment where people feel free to express their ideas without being judged. This also impacts morale and contributes towards better business and organisational results.

Igniters, those who have high confidence in this area, are generators of new, original solutions. They offer creative energy and novelty to the organisations in which they work. Often, they initiate new thinking and challenge the status quo, seeing how things could be done differently to achieve better results. Depending on their personality, they may be more risk-orientated, having less fear about trying out something new. Like *Identifiers*, *Igniters* tend to be future- and change-orientated. They provide the much-needed fuel for novelty that generates the initial spark for innovation to take place. *Ignite* is central to innovation for, without new ideas, innovation cannot happen.

THE IGNITER PROFILE

Innovation role – Providing novelty, freshness and energy for new ideas and a sense of new possibilities
Mindset – Creativity

Igniter's strengths:

1. The first to come up with new ideas
2. Good at seeking new knowledge outside their current areas of interest
3. Not afraid of challenging their own thinking as well as that of other people
4. Original thinkers
5. Can see connections between different and unrelated ideas
6. Good at creating a culture where people feel free to contribute their ideas
7. Skilled at motivating and inspiring others

*The swirling image illustrates the mindset of **Creativity**. The swirl moves backwards and forwards. It is open ended and explorative.*

Igniter's challenges

Igniters love to come up with new ideas. Lots of them. But as with all strengths, there can be challenges.

- They can become distracted with too many ideas that take them into multiple directions. This can dilute their energy and effectiveness.
- They can get attached to their own ideas and not think through whether they are feasible.
- They can enjoy jumping into action and implementation too quickly.
- They can generate lots of ideas and not see them through into fruition.

The challenge for *Igniters* is to harness their creative energy and work with other styles that could help bring their ideas to life. It is also helpful if they learn to stand back from their ideas to let them breathe before moving into action or, if they are less action-orientated, to choose and stick with an idea and start to think through how to make it work.

HOW TO COMMUNICATE WITH *IGNITERS*

Depending on the combination of 'I's on someone's profile, here are a few do's and don'ts that will help you communicate more effectively with *Igniters*.

Do's	**Don'ts**
Encourage them to talk about lots of different ideas, concepts and solutions	Be dismissive of their ideas or say they cannot work; be positive
Build on their ideas; say, 'Yes, and …', rather than 'Yes, but …'	Deconstruct their ideas too quickly; let their ideas have room to breathe
Involve them in brainstorming activities and workshops that will excite their mind and thinking	Involve them in detailed project planning and monitoring of activities and tasks
Talk about possibilities and opportunities to solve problems and challenges	Ask them to fulfil routine work that has little variety

THE IGNITE SKILLS

While there are many skills that help us to *Ignite* ideas, we will focus on six core attributes critical to this phase of innovation:

1 To generate lots of options and possiblities
2 To challenge assumptions
3 To see how ideas could be combined or connected
4 To be broadminded about learning new things
5 To stimulate others to contribute their ideas
6 To build a culture where there is freedom of expression

Let us look at each one in turn.

Throughout this chapter, I give examples and stories to help illustrate, and bring to life, this stage of innovation and practical ways, or activities and tools, to help you improve your ability and confidence to *ignite* ideas. Here is a top-line summary.

Skills	Tools	Activities
To generate lots of options and possiblities	Brainstorming	Spend time with creative people
To challenge assumptions		How to challenge your thinking
To see how ideas could be combined or connected	Parallel worlds Break the rules Random words	
To be broadminded about learning new things		Broaden your interests
To stimulate others to contribute their ideas		Ways to stimulate a creative environment
To build a culture where there is freedom of expression	Ways to increase your trust	Networks of trust

SKILL ONE – Being able to generate lots of options and possiblities

Back in the early 2000s, I worked as an innovation director in a research agency. We were responsible for helping big brands such as American Express, Coca-Cola, P&G, Diageo and Vodafone generate ideas and develop them into new products and services. What we discovered was that ideas could be greatly enhanced by including what we called 'Creative Consumers/Customers' – *ordinary people that purchased and used products or services from the category in which we wanted to innovate, who were also creative and could generate lots of ideas*. For example, when working with a beverages company to create new concepts, we involved creative, young men between the ages of 20–25 who liked to drink beer. The Creative Consumers were not there to critique or give their opinions on ideas that had already been generated, but to create them, in collaboration with the client, and, in so doing, challenge the client's way of thinking. Today, this practice often is referred to as co-creation – to co-create ideas and solutions for problems or opportunities with people outside of your organisation. The challenge is to find people who are creative as well as potential customers.

TOOLS

Brainstorming

1 Set up a brainstorming session. There is considerable evidence that the more ideas we have, the more likely we are to find a useful solution or answer.

2 Brainstorming is more than just bouncing ideas around, it actually has some rules.

3 Start a discussion about how you could involve creative consumers/customers in helping you generate new solutions. What could work in your context and how could you involve them in brainstorming sessions?

Rule	Activity
Rule 1: Go for Quantity.	Produce as many ideas as possible. The assumption is that the greater the number of ideas generated the bigger the chance of producing an affective solution.
Rule 2: Welcome Wild Ideas.	Generate ideas by challenging assumptions and looking from new perspectives. Wild ideas are encouraged.
Rule 3: Combine and Improve Ideas.	Combine new ideas to lead to more new ideas. This enhances divergent thinking, which can facilitate problem solving.
Rule 4: Withhold Criticism.	Do not allow discussion or questions during brainstorming. People will feel more willing to generate unusual ideas if they don't feel judged.

How to brainstorm properly

Source: Alex Faickney Osborn, often credited as the Father of Brainstorming

ACTIVITY

Spend time with an artistic person

Spend some time with an artist, writer, musician or someone else in the creative industries. Ask them about their work and how they generate new ideas. Some questions could include:

- What are your main sources of inspiration?
- What does your desk look like when you work? How does this affect you?
- How much time do you spend alone/with others?
- Do you write with a pen? Take notes in a journal? If so, does this help?
- How do your ideas take shape? Where do you think they come from?

Or, even better, start developing a creative practice for yourself (write, sing, dance or draw, etc.), and see if you start to think differently.

SKILL TWO – Being able to challenge assumptions

When I was a little girl, I used to love playing in the kitchen while my mum cooked dinner. I would empty the cupboards and take out the pots and pans, plastic bottles and containers and start to play. In my mind, the pots and pans were starships and rockets and all manner of imaginary things. Gradually, I stopped playing. I grew up. I had neatly filed into my brain that pots were for cooking, they were not starships after all.

As children, we make sense of the world by creating associations, or 'schemas'. These create the basis of the branching of our neurons in our brain. As we learn new things, our neurons develop like a tree and new branches are formed. The brain automatically sorts and files information according to these schemas. As we grow older, we are using the same pathways time and time again that become larger and deeper. The flow of new ideas starts to slow down but the flow of information speeds up. The brain becomes faster at classifying information by recognition and requires less and less reflection. This is why many adults find it hard to be creative. While there are great benefits to being able to look at an object and interpret its use in multiple ways, I would look silly now if I thought a pot was a starship. Therefore, when it comes to challenging the way that we think, the deep neural pathways, which allow us to process the world in a more efficient manner, simultaneously stop us from thinking differently.

There is a need for stimulus – a search for new experiences that jolt us into making new and unique connections. This could be anything that is not in our current pathway of thinking. It jolts us from one mental pathway to another and allows lateral connections, enabling the brain to create alternative ways of thinking.

ACTIVITY

Ways to challenge your thinking

1 Think of something that you really believe in and write down all the reasons for why you think it is true.

- Then imagine you held an opposite opinion and really believed that.

- Write down, or think through, all the reasons why you would hold that belief.
- Try and do this with as many different perspectives as you can.

2 Think over the last month. What have you read or heard that has challenged how you think?

- If you cannot think of anything, make it a goal this month to go out of your way to challenge your own thinking.
- At the end of each day, ask yourself, if I could live again today, what would I do differently and why?

3 Play. Release constraints on your imagination.

- Ask 'what if?' questions. Let yourself be a child again. Here are some examples to challenge your thinking: www.boardofinnovation.com/30-what-if-questions/

SKILL THREE – Being able to see how ideas could be combined or connected

Brain classification is an advantage as it allows us to handle a huge amount of data and information, but there are two big drawbacks to making such rapid classifications. First, the assumptions the brain makes can sometimes be wrong and cause us to jump to conclusions and make snap decisions about people or situations. Second, the way the brain processes information can inhibit creativity – every time we try to think of something new, the brain will use the same pathways. We get stuck in a rut. We cannot think out of the box. We find making new connections difficult.

Many of us are familiar with the terms right and left brain, right being responsible for creativity and left for logical analysis. While these terms are evolving and changing with the developments in neuroscience, it is important to be aware of how much time we spend doing tasks or activities that reinforce a particular way of thinking as this can inhibit our ability to make connections between ideas. Our societies, our schools and our work places largely reward logic, rational thinking, analysis, judgement and control. I have not known many organisations, or lived in many environments, which reward and reinforce daydreaming, emotion, art, colour, music, conversation and holistic ways of thinking. This is why it takes more effort; this is why it is often difficult to think differently. While the behaviours of judgement and control are necessary, in fact, even vital to innovation, they can kill off the early shoots of creativity that give an idea novelty.

TOOLS

Lateral thinking

Tool one – Parallel Worlds

1 Think of a brand, for example Apple.
2 On a flip chart or fresh piece of paper, write up all the words that you associate with the brand.
3 Then, take each word in turn and see if it can stimulate a fresh idea for your innovation challenge, i.e. Apple has simple, clear branding – what could your brand look like if you made it simpler to understand?

Tool two – Assumption Assassination/Break the Rules

1 Write up on a piece of paper all the rules or assumptions associated with your innovation challenge or insight.
2 Take each rule in turn and write down alternatives to that rule.

- For example, 'only people who have a lot of money can fly.'
- An assumption challenge would be 'what if we created a means to have low-cost travel?'
- This opened up new business models for low-cost airlines, breaking the assumptions of the given rules of the airline industry.

Example template

Rule/assumption	Broken rule	New idea
Only people who are rich can fly	What if we made flying cheaper for people who have less money?	Low-cost airlines (which stripped out costs associated with expensive travel)

Tool three – Random Words

1 Think about something that has nothing to do with your challenge – examples could include objects, words or pictures.
2 Put the object, word or picture alongside your innovation challenge.
3 Does it stimulate any fresh connections or spark any new ideas?

DID YOU KNOW?

Dr Paul Torrance, an American psychologist and pioneer in creativity research, found, in a range of longitudinal studies, that the characteristics of creative thinking differed from intelligence and logical reasoning. In fact, he found, the use of intelligence tests to identify gifted students misses about 70 per cent of those who are equally gifted using creativity criteria. Torrance believed creativity could be taught by providing environments that encourage 'exploring, questioning, experimenting, manipulating, rearranging things, testing and modifying, listening, looking, feeling – and then thinking about it – incubating' (Torrance, 1995).

There have been other interesting studies conducted, one about how our creativity declines with age. A longitudinal study by George Land and Beth Jarman tracked 1,600 children from the age of 3 to 15. What do you think they found? By the age of 15, those scoring in the creative genius level, measured by eight lateral thinking tests, had dropped from 98 per cent to 10 per cent, and 200,000 adults that took the same tests scored only 2 per cent. This means that, by the time young people are entering the workforce, a lot of their natural creativity has diminished.

If you do not think of yourself as particularly creative, the good news that this research identifies is that we can learn to be more creative and, if we lead or manage others, we can help to create an environment that stimulates creative thinking.

SKILL FOUR — Being broadminded about learning new things

We are all familiar with the term 'thinking out of the box', but what is *the box*? The box is made up of our experience, perceptions and knowledge of how we make sense of things. It is our worldview. It is relatively easy to have ideas within a domain in which we are interested or have experience, as there is familiarity, knowledge and comfort in what is already known. While there is nothing inherently wrong in this, when we are trying to innovate, we need to think outside of what already exists. Brain classification does not help us here either, as we get stuck with what we know. This is the box that we need to break out of. Coupled with this is the human tendency to conform to group culture – normal or expected behaviour. If we challenge what is deemed to be right, correct and proper, then we will be seen as an outsider to the group. This causes a big dilemma in organisations as they need to cultivate creativity and curiosity in their employees, but they also want them to obey the rules. Organisations have largely been built for efficiency and growth and have rewarded people who can implement plans and drive productivity. Again, there is nothing necessarily wrong in this but, if we want to cultivate new thinking, we have to challenge what already exists, in ourselves, as well as the organisations and societies in which we work and live.

ACTIVITY

Broaden your interests

1 Do an audit of your current interests, experience and knowledge.
   - See if there is a connection you can make between one of your interests and your innovation challenge.
   - Can this inspire a new idea?

2 Find a friend or a colleague who has an interest in a hobby or topic that you know nothing about.
   - Ask them about it. Why do they find it interesting?
   - What have you learnt?

3 Take a task or activity that you do the same way, over and over again. Do it differently.
   - If you go to work or another destination using the same route, find a new way that you have not been before.
   - Go out of your way to get lost.

4 Think of your innovation challenge or insight – are there other organisations, or individuals, trying to solve similar problems, but in different areas?
   - What can you learn from their approaches?
5 This week, challenge yourself to learn two new things.

The brain needs new inputs to draw from in order to create ideas. As you build these approaches into your daily living, you will find random thoughts start to percolate and images, words and ideas will appear and start to stimulate new thinking.

SKILL FIVE – Being able to stimulate others to contribute their ideas

Have you ever shared an idea with a colleague only to have it shot down? If that happens over and over again, I can guarantee you will stop sharing your ideas with this person. Yet, ideas are the fuel of innovation. So, what makes us share our ideas with some people and not others? Maybe the person is open-minded and curious, maybe they are great at building on our ideas to make them better and maybe they are influential and willing to support us. It could be a lot of things, but fundamental to this relationship – particularly at the early stages of innovation when ideas are often raw and undefined – is the sense of feeling safe and being heard.

In one of my previous roles, I was hired to help an organisation to become more customer focused. Energy and enthusiasm was in the air and there was a great feeling of new possibility. Within two years, I, and many other people, had left. Despite being hired specifically for our creativity, the culture just did not support it. If I heard, 'Oh, we have tried that before', 'That will never work', 'A great idea, but it will never get approval', once, I heard it many times. The most creative person can be stifled in their creativity if their work environments are not supportive of new ideas. We can think of these behaviours as a bit soft, yet the atmosphere in which people work, generated often by the behaviour of managers, is fundamental to getting the best out of people, which, ultimately, affects motivation.

Ways to stimulate a creative environment

1 When someone comes to you to share an idea, instead of saying, 'I like it but ...' practise saying, 'I like it and ...' Catch yourself and others, if you think someone's idea is being criticised.

2 Practise saying *yes*, we can do that instead of *no* we can't do that.

3 If you are a manager or a leader, look out for the people who have a natural way of motivating and facilitating others and support the development of this skill. Encourage people who are natural catalysts for innovation by giving them opportunities to help motivate others.

4 Watch this film with your team and discuss how you can cultivate more *Purpose*, *mastery* and *autonomy* in your working culture: www.youtube.com/watch?v=u6XAPnuFjJc

5 Look at how you are working. Are there places you can create where people can naturally congregate, connect and share ideas? Physical, collaborative space is also important to culture building.

6 Try 'walking work' – design a specific topic you want to discuss with someone or your team and set 30 minutes to discuss it, outside of your office or working environment in the outdoors. At the end of 30 minutes, discuss your ideas. Did being outside help?

7 Eat fresh snacks that stimulate the brain. Here are 10 of the best you can try: https://idesigni.co.uk/blog/10-of-the-best-brain-foods-for-creativity/

8 Learn from companies who have an innovative culture: in *Century of Innovation*, a book about 3M's history, four key ingredients were considered important in fostering a culture of innovation:

- Attracting and retaining imaginative and productive people
- Creating a challenging environment
- Designing an organisation that does not get in people's way
- Offering rewards that nourish both self-esteem and personal bank accounts

What can you learn from 3M?

SKILL SIX – Being able to create a culture where there is freedom of expression

A couple of years ago, I attended a conference in New York on neuroleadership, where thought leaders from the world of neuroscience and leadership development came together to explore what science can teach us about how we lead people and develop innovative places to work. One of the guest speakers, Dr Karen Stephenson, a leading expert in the field of social network analysis (SNA), opened my thinking to why organisations find it so hard to build and sustain a culture of innovation. Innovation can be in your mission statement, hanging on the wall or listed as one of your top organisational values – but if trust is not being cultivated within the flow of work, innovation will be eroded, diluted or even completely stalled, no matter the wishes of senior management. It is one thing to have new ideas yourself, but if you can create a culture where others feel free to share their ideas, you are able to leverage this skill beyond your own capability.

Work does not necessarily flow through neatly designed organisational charts. It flows randomly and spontaneously through people talking, listening, supporting and challenging each other in different parts of the company. The power these key connectors have is given, not taken. It is given by their numerous trusted relationships with people around them – and, more often than not, senior vice-president will not be on their business card. Want to cultivate innovation? It will not happen if you are asking people to submit or share ideas that are killed off quietly by other power brokers that insist on preserving the status quo. From our experience in working with Dr Stephenson, the organisations that are starting to see the power of harnessing key trust relationships are the ones who have a head start in building and sustaining a culture of innovation.

ACTIVITY

Ways to increase your trust

1 Being reliable and dependable are two key elements of trust building. This week, make sure, if you promise someone you will do something that you follow up, otherwise do not commit.

2 When someone shares an idea with you, be conscious of how you are responding. Build on the idea, rather than criticising it, by saying, 'What I like about that is …' Remain open to other people's ideas.

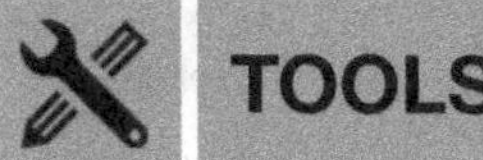

TOOLS

Networks of trust

On a piece of paper, write your name in the middle and then write up all the names of people that you share new ideas with.

1 Draw a thin line between yourself and others for low trust and a thick line for high trust.
2 If you contact the person a lot, draw a shorter line.
3 How many trusted relationships do you have?
4 Are you overly reliant on one or two people? If so, try to develop other relationships. Reconnect with someone you have not spoken to for a long time. For example, in the drawing here, person A is trusted but not contacted very often, person D is highly trusted and contacted a lot, maybe too much. This person could strengthen their relationship with person E, who is not as close but does have a medium level of trust.

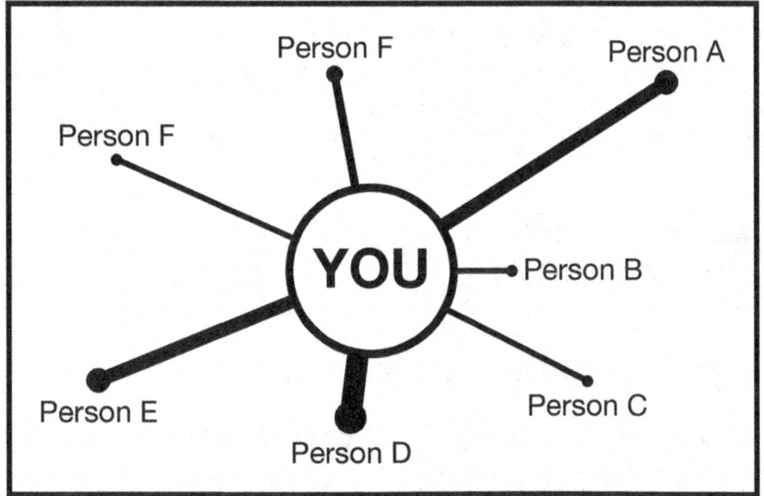

Dangers of Missing Out the *IGNITE* Stage

- You (or your team) may generate ideas that lack creativity and novelty.
- You generate ideas but they are unadventurous and shallow.
- You end up producing outcomes that may lack depth and innovation impact.
- Ideas generated may solve only incremental challenges.

The ability to *ignite* requires diversity, diverse thinking, diverse inputs and perspectives. How can you encourage more? To dig deeper into developing the skill set of *ignite*, refer to the resource guide at the end of this chapter.

THE IGNITE MINDSET

'AN ORIENTATION AND ATTITUDE THAT DESIRES TO SEEK AND IMAGINE NEW POSSIBILITIES'

CREATIVITY

When was the last time you browsed the magazine shelves looking at really cool design magazines, walked a labyrinth or attended a laughing club? Odd questions, you may muse, but not according to Daniel Pink, author of *A Whole New Mind: Why Right-Brainers Will Rule the Future*. Mr Pink's main argument is that our socialisation, education and training have prepared us well for the world we used to live in, which required high doses of sequential, left-brain thinking; or, in overly simplistic terms, planning, analysis, writing and arithmetic. But it is not doing such a good job at preparing us for the future. A future which, I might add, has already arrived. This requires a different type of thinking, a whole new mind altogether. We have to cultivate and unleash the contextual right side of our brain, largely responsible for dreaming, recognition of faces, emotion and creativity and combine it with the power of our left. We need to develop a *creative* mindset.

Creativity, or the use of the imagination to develop original ideas, is the fuel of innovation for, without being creative, we will not generate new combinations of ideas that eventually could turn into innovations. Sadly, for a lot of us, our creative and imaginative minds have slowly eroded as we have grown older and we find it harder and harder to generate new ideas. But there is hope! We can, with the use of fresh experiences, new knowledge and creativity tools, start to think more creatively and imaginatively.

BEYOND THE RIGHT AND LEFT BRAIN

Writer Elizabeth Gilbert, in her book *Big Magic*, likens creativity to an essence, as if it is seeking a host, a person or people to collaborate with so that it can bring itself into the material world. To life. This metaphor speaks of receptivity and being an open vessel to receive creative insight and inspiration for what may emerge. This is probably why the subconscious mind plays such a vital role, and also why a lot of creative people say that ideas seem to come from 'nowhere'. Ideas land in their minds and, only when acted on within the imagination, do they start to take shape.

While the distinction between right and left brain is a bit outdated, particularly with modern discoveries in neuroscience and the role of our subconscious mind, it is still a useful concept to help us think about the types of activities we could do to help develop a creative mindset, retrain our brain, so that, even if we think we are predominantly left brained, ideas will start to 'come out of nowhere'. This table gives a useful checklist of functions that are normally associated with the different parts of the brain.

Left Brain	Right Brain
Time	Geometric patterns
Words	Faces
Self control	Emotional expression
Logic	Intuition
Language	Non-language sounds

Judgement	Music
Sequence	Conversation
Verbal memory	Non-verbal memory
Lists	Daydreaming
Analysis	Creativity
Reading	Distance
Competition	Colour
Sports	Art
Coordination	Shapes

A great story of ideas coming from random places is the invention of VELCRO®, a fastener for clothes or other items. VELCRO® consists of two strips of material, one covered with tiny loops and the other with tiny flexible hooks, which, when pressed together, stick to each other. It was invented by Swiss engineer George de Mestral after he removed burrs that kept sticking to his clothes and his dog's fur when walking in the Alps. De Mestral wondered how the tiny hooks of the cockle-burs (the seed packets produced by burdock, which are covered with stiff spines) were sticking to him. He took the specimen home and examined the tiny hooks at the ends of the burr's projections under a microscope and he observed an interlocking mechanism that inspired him to consider: could a series of small-scale, interlocking hooks have a practical application in clothes? This inspired him to create the now ubiquitous VELCRO®.

If you remember, we talked about different creativity tools in the skills section of this chapter. The inspiration for VELCRO® was similar to the creativity tool – Random Words. Two unrelated concepts came together to spark a new idea.

While often we equate being creative with artists, musicians, writers and other people in the 'creative professions', we need to start challenging this way of thinking and realise that all of us, to some degree or another, have the ability to be creative and, if it does not feel that natural to us, we can develop a more creative mindset, in ourselves and others around us. Any time we are faced with challenges or dilemmas, we need creative thinking. Creativity is what makes innovation innovative, it is new ways of thinking or combining elements into something that didn't exist before. I like to think of innovation as a practice as well as a process or an event. If we think of innovation as a practice, then we need to start experimenting with new ways of thinking – not only for innovation events or projects at work, but in our everyday life, every day.

The potent ingredients of open mindedness with concentrated effort, the marriage of creativity and discipline and the observation of the ordinary linked with imagination are small ways we can do this. Something unexpected starts to happen. Ideas pop out of nowhere or, suddenly, you have inspiration for a problem you are trying to solve. It is as if, in this type of practice, something unlocks in the brain. So, developing the orientation, the mindset of creativity as a form of practice, is where we need to begin.

These Activities outlined below will help to spark creative thinking and show you a fresh perspective on life. They do not have to be difficult or expensive. The important thing is to carve out space for yourself to support the development of this mindset, orientation and way of thinking, not just in your work, but in your life in general. This will help develop a creative mindset and allow you to tap into the power of your subconscious mind to help improve the way you create and, therefore, innovate.

While the mindsets of *curiosity* and *creativity* are both fundamental to innovation because of their expansive and open ways of thinking, and their ability to originate and generate new ideas, it does not stop here. This brings us to the third 'I' of The Six 'I's of Innovation®, which we will explore in the next chapter of the book – *investigate*.

Want to Develop a Creative Mindset?

An orientation and attitude that intentionally allows the mind to wander, seek and imagine new connections or possibilities.

TRY THIS

1 Inspired by artist Julia Cameron's *Morning Pages* – write three pages of longhand writing, yes, with a pen, every morning. Let your mind wander and see where your imagination takes you. Three pages too long? Try one page to start.

2 Once a month, take yourself out on an Artist's Date – do something you think might help spark creativity. For example, I have made trips to

different galleries, attended storytelling workshops, blown the dust off my old guitar and played tunes I knew from years ago, gone for long walks along the beach, in forests and parks and walked slowly without a goal in mind. Allow yourself to day dream.

3 Here are some other activities that will help develop a creative mindset:
   - Dance without moving your feet.
   - Ask a child to teach you something.
   - Practise creative visualisation.
   - Daydream for 15 minutes.
   - Run for pleasure not exercise.
   - Create a personal logo.
   - Go into a dream-like state.
   - Picture your life five years from now and create a collage of images.
   - Fly a kite.
   - Play with modelling clay.

Make these *creativity* mindset activities part of your life.

Ready to move on to *investigate*? Use this simple checklist to make sure you have covered some of the most salient points of *ignite*.

Activity	Complete
I have developed and tested insights that are based on real people's needs.	
I have generated new ideas using lateral thinking tools and brainstorming techniques.	
I have broadened my network and developed a new trust relationship that will help me innovate.	
I have practised some right-brain activities to expand my imagination and creative mindset.	

To dig deeper into developing the skill set, refer to the resources guide at the end of this chapter, but, first, let us meet Marco Brabec, whose highest score on The Six 'I's® is *ignite*.

LET'S MEET MARCO BRABEC

THE IGNITER PROFILE

Name:	Marco Brabec
Job:	MD Cisco Systems, Services Delivery
	Lead Partner Engagement Team, Switzerland
Company:	Cisco Systems
Primary Six 'I's® rating:	Igniter

What challenge are you looking to solve with innovation right now?

I think our biggest challenge is the readiness of the organisation to innovate, particularly when things are going well, why change things? We do change a lot but often the change is operationally focused and not innovation driven. Yet, if we don't generate new ways of doing things, even when business is good, we will become complacent and our competitors will pass us by. A big part of our strategy is business model innovation in the area of service transformation. We are traditionally a product- and sales-led organisation that has provided networking and communication infrastructure as our core business. A lot of that is non-recurring business. Our goal is to double our sales revenue, over the next three years, in the area of recurring business, such as services and software. This is going to take a lot of new ideas and a commitment to doing things differently.

Looking at your Six 'I's® results, you're an *igniter*. How does this knowledge impact or change the way you work?

As an *igniter*, I enjoy and see the relevance of generating new ideas. I also see my role in creating a team environment for others to do this as well. This does require managing the tension between delivering what the business needs today, and what it will need tomorrow, but I am willing to do this. I believe it is important. There can be reluctance amongst others to lead this way, probably because they are worried that it will distract their team from focusing on immediate business results. There is always a fine line between these two elements, and keeping them in balance is difficult to achieve, but I am more aware of it now.

How do you play to your strengths? What advice would you give other people who want to get better at *igniting* ideas?

If I am not playing to my strengths, I get bored, so I seek new ways to give expression to this strength by contributing and volunteering to be part of work groups and task forces that are outside my core work environment. I read a lot. I learn from others who are innovative. My advice to others is to do the same. Broaden your horizons from what is immediately important to you. Talk to more people inside and outside your organisation. You will then start to make connections between different ideas that are unrelated and this will help to spark new ideas.

What steps, if any, would you take to improve the areas where you are not so strong, or that are important to you and how?

I don't think one can, or should be, good at everything. I manage a global team with members in Asia, Europe, Australia and the USA. I have made a conscious decision to recruit for diversity in skills and experience. What is important is to have a team where people can complement my skills as well as each other's. I also learn from those who are good at *investigating* to see how they approach things and how they do things differently from me. This helps me grow my awareness and skills and helps me see my blind spots.

How has The Six 'I's® helped you and your teams/business? What examples, if any, can you share?

We have been working with The Six 'I's® over several years now and have applied it on a variety of business challenges. These have ranged from increasing our margins by improving relationships with colleagues in our IT call centres about how we allocate project roles and responsibilities, to creating new ways of engaging customers in our key accounts through quarterly business reviews and other practices. It gives us a structured process. A lot of people think that innovation is just about sparking a new idea out of the blue, and they struggle with being able to do this. The Six 'I's® has broadened this concept and helped my team see that they can all contribute to creating value for the organisation.

Have you produced something you would consider innovative?

Currently we are working on new business model innovation in service delivery. We realise we lack the capability to develop and deliver managed services through a channel partner framework. This is an exciting space for the company to explore. Applying The Six 'I's® has helped us to realise what our own limitations are as well as *identify* the external opportunity for driving new sources of growth and *igniting* new solutions. It has given us a step-by-step approach to think things through, get clarity and *investigate* our ideas more thoroughly to see if they will work before we *invest* more time and resources.

THE IGNITE RESOURCE GUIDE

This chapter outlines some resources for further exploration to help you get better at igniting ideas and developing the mindset of creativity.

RESOURCE GUIDE

Whether creativity comes naturally to you or not, developing practices to help open your thinking and make you more receptive will enhance your ability to think laterally. This will help you to, be more divergent and see connections between different ideas. Here are a few additional resources and practices I have found useful.

- **A Whole New Mind.** For those of us who love practical 'how-to', as well as brain science and convincing arguments for why this is important, Daniel Pink's book *A Whole New Mind* gives great tips and suggestions. He outlines six areas that we need to cultivate: design, story, symphony, empathy, play and meaning, with detailed 'portfolios' on how to develop each one. His newsletter is good, too: www.danpink.com
- **Journaling.** I have written journals, reflections on myself and life, since I was a young child and have found the practice of journaling, writing by hand in a notebook, as a source of great inspiration for new ideas. It also helps to stop, take note of what is occurring and build awareness of self, others and the world around us. I encourage everyone I teach to keep a journal. Here is a great site that will tell you everything you need to know to get started: www.journalingsaves.com/welcome/

- **Creativity workshop.** With the proliferation of online training programmes, learning about any subject that may be of interest is easy and cost-effective. One programme I particularly enjoyed on creativity was Elizabeth Gilbert's Creativity Workshop on Udemy: www.udemy.com/elizabeth-gilberts-creativity-workshop/
- **Creativity test.** Want to find out how creative you are? Complete the Torrance Tests of Creative Thinking (TTCT): www.ststesting.com/ngifted.html
- **Right- and left-brain assessment.** While there are lots of freebies to test how right or left brained you are, if you want to have a comprehensive and validated assessment, this is the company to visit: www.herrmannsolutions.com
- **50 creative websites.** Here is a fabulous resource for 50 websites that will inspire creativity www.creativeboom.com/resources/50-of-the-best-websites-for-daily-inspiration/
- **Mind tools.** This site is a great resource for all manner of thinking tools. They also have a resource guide specifically aimed at boosting creativity in self and in teams: www.mindtools.com/pages/main/newMN_CT.htm
- **Learn to draw.** Never thought you could draw? Betty Edwards can teach you how: http://drawright.com
- **Social network theory.** For more information about Dr Karen Stephenson's work, visit www.drkaren.us

FURTHER READING

There are numerous books on creativity, here are some that I have enjoyed and found useful:

Buzan, T. (2003) *Head First: 10 Ways to Tap into Your Natural Genius*. Thorsons.

Catmul, E. (2014) *Creativity, Inc.: Overcoming the Unseen Forces That Stand in the Way of True Inspiration*. Random House.

Csikszentmihalyi, M. (2013) *Creativity: Flow and the Psychology of Discovery and Invention*. Harper Perennial.

Jarvis, J. (2011) *What would Google Do? Reverse-Engineering the Fastest Growing Company in the History of the World*. Harper Business.

Kahneman, D. (2013) *Thinking, Fast and Slow*. Farrar, Straus and Giroux.

Michalko, M. (2006) *Thinkertoys: A Handbook of Creative-Thinking Techniques*. Ten Speed Press.

Pink, D. (2008) *A Whole New Mind; Why Right Brainers Will Rule the Future*. Marshall Cavendish.

Singh, K. *Thinking Hats and Coloured Turbans*. Pearson.

INVESTIGATE

PROTOTYPE, TEST AND RESEARCH IDEAS

'That is great, Natalie,' the man said as he closed down his laptop. 'Let me get back to you with some ideas on how we can move this forward, it's certainly what we need right now, I just have to figure out how we can make it work.' I walked out of the room, a big smile on my face. Wow, what a conversation! We had discussed and explored a range of subjects and I was sure that a decision had just been made to move ahead with our proposal.

Somehow, I had thought that because I had *identified* a need for organisational innovation – or the building of capabilities, skills and structures to help a company innovate – that there would be a clear market for it, as in people would buy the service. Back in 2006, this was just not the case. I had not really *investigated* the idea. I had *identified* a need and *ignited* some ideas, but I had not thought through how it could really work. While individuals inside an organisation might have seen the need, and managed to find funding, most organisations were just not structured or designed in a way that allowed them to take action, even if they wanted to.

In 2006, I had not really appreciated the relatively young professional status that the discipline of innovation has within organisational life. Unlike marketing, finance, operations or the sales department, which are all common business functions, whom do you call when you want to talk about innovation? Who owns innovation? Not just research and development or the development of new products or services, but ownership around making innovation part of everyone's day job. It is a question that usually receives a blank response. Yet, pick up any business magazine and, invariably, you will find multiple articles on the strategic importance of innovation for a company's growth. A PricewaterhouseCoopers report highlighted 72 per cent of CEOs stating innovation as one of their top three priorities. So, certainly there was an *identified* need, but it did require a bit more investigation to explore how the ideas could work.

Thankfully, it is getting easier now as more and more directors inside organisations see the need for rapid ways to deploy innovative products, services and business models and this means building up skills and internal capabilities to execute this. One of our clients is Singapore Airlines and, I must say, it is one of the few companies that I have met where different parts of the organisation have come together to think systematically about how they innovate – the head of HR, the head of new product development and the head of research, as well as a number of other departmental heads, but this is rare.

This story illustrates a couple of very important lessons – good ideas, even if they are focused on real needs and are even useful, will work only if the market – customers – are ready and able to buy. We need to stand back and look at the broader context of how an idea can go to market and test it thoroughly. It means thinking things through, carefully and systematically, and not just jumping feet first into *implementation*. The need for a *critical* mindset so we can *investigate* new ideas and improve their likelihood of success is the subject of this chapter.

Throughout, I will give examples, stories, activities and tools to help you improve your ability and confidence to *investigate* new ideas.

The *investigate* phase is central to innovation, as it can save a lot of time, resources and money by not jumping in too quickly to make an idea happen. This includes systematically researching, analysing and assessing ideas and ensuring that ideas are useful, not just novel. This also incorporates design thinking or customer-centred approaches to creating new solutions. This is really important, as open innovation – the use of external as well as internal ideas and paths to market – will help to ensure that what is being offered is going to create value for those that will use the service, product or process.

Having a culture where exploration and questioning is encouraged and getting other people to think things through carefully and systematically are important leadership and culture-building skills, as they help to create an environment where people have permission to explore, test and prototype – a sample, model or release of a product built to test a concept or process. They also help to encourage people to research whether ideas will work before further commitment is invested.

This phase of innovation requires a *critical* mindset that can help you to stand back from your ideas so that you can think them through.

THE INVESTIGATOR PROFILE

Innovation role – Providing analytical thinking and objectivity
Mindset – Critical

Investigator's strengths:

1. Systematically researching, analysing and assessing ideas
2. Making sure ideas are useful, not just novel
3. Understanding the importance of testing and validating ideas before moving into implementation
4. Being willing to test their thinking with customers and stakeholders
5. Creating a culture where exploration and questioning is encouraged
6. Encouraging other people to think things through carefully and systematically

*The image illustrates the mindset of Investigate, **Critical**. The orientation, whilst still exploratory, needs to start to converge and be more analytical in approach.*

Investigator's challenges

Being analytical is one of the strengths of an investigator, but sometimes their strengths can backfire.

- They may continually search for more validation before they are willing to make a commitment. This can lead to a new initiative getting immobilised or stuck
- They can get lost in the detail and lose sight of the bigger picture; why they are innovating and the overall PURPOSE
- They can be dismissive of ideas if they don't think they are feasible, being too quick to judge something that is untried or tested

Investigators need to make sure that, in their research, testing and analysis, they do not lose the originality of the idea, but instead experiment with it to improve its likelihood of success. If not, the novelty that once made it unique, and possibly innovative, could be lost.

HOW TO COMMUNICATE WITH *INVESTIGATORS*

Depending on the combination of 'I's on someone's profile, here are a few do's and don'ts that will help you communicate more effectively with *investigators*.

Do's	Don'ts
Talk about detail and be thorough in your approach	Be haphazard or lack rigour and logic
Encourage them to test their ideas with customers or those who would be involved in refining ideas	Jump into action without finding out whether the idea meets a customer or market need
Present your ideas in a systematic way and invite critical thinking	Be overly attached to an idea just because you created it; be willing to stand back and invite scrutiny; see their critical thinking as helpful
Make space for them to research and explore an idea with depth	Crowd their thinking with too many ideas without giving them time to explore

THE INVESTIGATE SKILLS

While there are many skills that help us to *investigate* ideas, we will focus on six core attributes critical to this phase of innovation:

1 To be analytical and structured
2 To work things through carefully and methodically
3 To involve customers and those who would benefit from an idea
4 To make sure the idea has potential to meet a real need
5 To help others be more methodical and organised in their thinking
6 To create an envivornment where people are encouraged to explore and question

Let us look at each one in turn.

Below is a top-line summary of the skills and a selection of tools and activities for the area of *investigate*.

Skills	Tools	Activities
To be analytical and structured	Develop a selection criteria	Insert the pause button
To work things through carefully and methodically	Proposition development The Three Horizons	Research questions
To involve customers and those who would benefit from an idea	Design Thinking	
To make sure the idea has potential to meet a real need	Prototyping	Research methods
To help others be more methodical and organised in their thinking	Six Thinking Hats®	
To create an envivornment where people are encouraged to explore and question		Ask good questions

SKILL ONE – Being able to be analytical and structured

Investigate has been one of my lowest areas of strength. Despite having a background in research, and being highly analytical, my core strengths are in the area of *identify* and *ignite*. I like to explore opportunities and generate new ideas. Speed is of the essence. I am impatient. I want to move into action. As the Nike brand says, 'Just Do It'. While laudable in some ways, this can lack objectivity or standing back and testing to see if an idea is a really good idea. My friend and colleague Lillian Ing, a clinical psychologist who has been working with us using The Six 'I's® Model, helped shift my mindset by reframing how I saw the *investigate* phase of innovation. She said a wonderful thing that has stuck with me ever since. 'Insert the pause'. Stop, take a breath, look at what you are doing, can it be done better or differently, is the idea going to help you meet your *Purpose*? I am learning to love this space now of investigation and holding the often tricky balance between being passionate and detached.

As The Six 'I's® profiling tool measures self-perception of skills, it is possible to retake the assessment and track changes over time. I have retaken the assessment several times over the past few years and have noticed an improvement in my scores as I have consciously built my *investigate* skills.

Contrary to popular opinion, some ideas are not good ideas. We need to be willing to be dispassionate, particularly about ideas that are our own, and be able to stand back and analyse and assess them and, if necessary, put them on hold, wait for the right time, improve them or let them go.

ACTIVITY

Insert the pause button

Noun: a temporary stop in action or speech.

Synonyms: cessation, break, check, lull, respite, breathing space, hiatus, gap, interlude.

1. Print up the definition of a pause or write it down. Place it somewhere where you will see it frequently.
2. Pause.
3. Repeat.

Develop a selection criteria

1 Think of criteria by which you want to assess your ideas, particularly if you have a lot of ideas and you are not quite sure what to focus on. Create 'selection criteria'. These could include elements such as:

Area	Description
Novelty	To what degree is the idea different, or unique?
Relevance	Will it help to adress your PURPOSE?
Potential Return on Investment	Will it potentially add more value than cost?
Ease of Implementation	How difficult will it be to implement time, resource and manpower?
Desirability	Is this something that a customer really wants and is willing to pay for and use?
Scalability	Is it easy to replicate, or scale? Is it sustainable?

2 Rank your ideas using your selection criteria and analyse and assess them. Be careful not to drop the novel ones and just pick the ones that are easy to implement. If you do this, then the innovative aspect of your idea will be lost. *Investigate* how you can make the novel ideas work.

The Three Horizons

The Three Horizons, featured in the book *The Alchemy of Growth* (Baghai, Coley and White), is a very useful way of thinking about the potential impact of an idea that you are creating. It also helps to give a framework for a range of innovations – from the incremental, small changes to how things are being done, to the more radical – innovations which change or create new markets and business models.

Horizon 1 – This horizon represents 'business as usual'. As change occurs, what exists starts to feel out of place or no longer fit for Purpose. This is where more smaller steps or incremental innovation starts to take place.

Horizon 2 – This horizon is where new opportunities for doing things quite differently start to emerge. It is often one of the most difficult areas to innovate in as it requires holding the balance of what is needed today, while looking to the future.

Horizon 3 – This is the horizon where radical innovation occurs. Completely new ways of doing things that are very different to the status quo disrupt and create new opportunities for change.

1 Look at your ideas.
2 What type of innovation Horizon do they belong to?
3 What are the implications for how you manage current performance while maximising future opportunities for growth? Your idea will need different types of management depending on what Horizon it belongs to.

Idea	Horizon 1	Horizon 2	Horizon 3	Implications

SKILL TWO – Being able to work things through carefully and methodically

Innovating is an iterative process. What I mean by this is that you will go backwards and forwards, particularly around the first three 'I's – *identify*, *ignite* and *investigate* as you seek to work out what the opportunity is and what solutions will best meet the needs that you are trying to address. As it can be quite unpredictable, develop a systematic way of thinking things through. If we want to bring ideas into the world, they need to be robust and based on real insights, not just random good ideas that cannot be developed or used. This means being clear on how you articulate your idea, the need it is addressing and the components of how it will work. A term often used in the business world is value proposition design. So, what is a proposition?

A proposition is a way to capture and communicate an idea to the people you want to engage with, based on their needs. It describes the core of an idea, its benefits and why the person should buy, or use the solution, you are proposing.

In three words it communicates relevancy, uniqueness and value. You need to think it through and keep honing the value proposition until it is easy to understand and communicate.

Research:

1 Your competition (what are they offering that is similar)
2 Your market place (how ready is it for what you want to offer)
3 Your potential customers or users (does it address their needs)

ACTIVITY

Research questions

Think through the best way for you to systematically research your ideas.

1 Who do you need to talk to?
   - Where do you need to find out more information?
   - What experts can help you accelerate your learning?
   - What is your competition offering?

TOOLS

Proposition development

Pick one of the stronger insights that you have developed and an idea that you think will address the need you have isolated. Have a go at writing your own proposition. Use the following table as a guide.

Element	Description
Insight	What is the customer/market need and barrier to it being met?
Benefit	What is the end benefit you are offering? Capture it in one short sentence.
Sub-headline	Outline a specific explanation of what you offer, for whom and why.
Three bullet points	List the key benefits or features.
Include a visual element	Show an image and reinforce your main message.

SKILL THREE – Being able to involve customers and those who would benefit from an idea

The term *design thinking*, popularised in the business world by the Californian design company, IDEO, is becoming a more accepted practice and approach for the creation and development of new solutions in many organisations. It is a person-centred, prototype-driven process for innovation that can be applied to different areas such as products, services, processes and business model design. Design Thinking incorporates the ability to combine empathy, creativity and rationality to meet customer needs. Empathy is a very important skill for us to develop if we want to innovate more effectively. It is about feeling with people, not for them; it is about making connection, and seeing the world from their perspective. One way we can practise this is through observing and interviewing others – learning about those for whom we want to innovate, generating solutions, building prototypes or representations of the solution and testing them out with the people that will use them. This requires us to get out of our meeting rooms, beyond the borders of our organisations and observe, understand and engage with those for whom we want to provide new solutions. This will help to ensure that what is being created is going to have value.

TOOLS

Design thinking

Apply a Design Thinking approach to your innovation challenge:

1 Observe and interview potential customers (*identify*).
2 Create insights (*identify*).
3 Generate ideas for new solutions (*ignite*).
4 Build prototypes or representations of your ideas and solutions and test them out with the people that will use them (*investigate*), iterate and improve.

Design Thinking, empathy building and how to observe others are very rich subjects in and of themselves and many people are specialists in these fields. There are many comprehensive books on these subjects. The important thing for you to remember, as you innovate at work, is to think about how to apply these approaches to create rich and compelling solutions that will add value to your customers and help you to achieve your goals.

DID YOU KNOW?

Airbnb, an online business that enables home owners to share rooms with travellers, started as yet another bed and breakfast startup in the loft of its founders, but it was on the verge of bust when revenues plummeted to $200 per week in 2009. The three founders, along with their first investor, decided to do some brainstorming to find out the problem. One reason, they discovered, was the lack of quality images on their website. So, they packed their bags, rented a camera, visited places and replaced the poor-quality images with beautiful high-resolution ones. This doubled their revenues within a week.

As their mentality shifted, they realised they needed to go out, meet customers and come up with clever real-world solutions. Airbnb went ahead to embed a design-thinking approach everywhere in the company. Airbnb employees take a trip in their first or second week after joining. They capture customer struggles by venturing into their shoes and document their experience to share with other employees. New employees are asked to come up with new features on their first day at the company and every employee is encouraged to come up with innovative ideas.

Source: Pankaj – https://inkoniq.com/blog/how-design-thinking-transforming-the-world-and-lives-of-millions/

What this story can illustrate is that it is important not to try to create solutions in isolation from those that may eventually benefit from them. You need to meet customers, or potential customers, not assume that just because you have a good idea it will work. Sometimes, the solutions do not have to be world breaking, they can be small ideas that have a significant impact – like the improvement that high-quality photographs had on the Airbnb website.

SKILL FOUR – Being able to make sure the idea has potential to meet a real need

Remember the definition of an idea, outlined at the beginning of the book. *An idea is a thought or suggestion as to a possible course of action that generates in the mind.* An idea is not an innovation. A lot has to happen before an idea can move into being deemed innovative and this is really important to remember. If we just jump from idea (*ignite*) into implementation, then we miss out the critical stage of finding out whether our idea is useful, not just novel. This is why developing a proposition, an outline of what you want to develop and why it will be useful, is so necessary at this stage. Go back to *skill two* and find out how. There can be a temptation, once you have an idea, just to start developing it in isolation to the people that might use it without ever showing them what it is you want to offer.

Research methods

Look at the proposition that you have written. What is the best way to test and research it? Depending on what you have created, there are many ways to research and test your ideas. They could include:

- Focus groups
- Depth interviews
- In situ testing
- Surveys

TOOLS

Prototyping

Develop a prototype. There are a number of ways to test a prototype:

- A mock-up of a product
- A story board
- An illustration
- A web application or test website
- A mock-up of a service offering
- A customer experience design
- An advertisement

Pilots or trial offers of your solution can also help to test a proposition in real time to see how it works and what people think. This is a particularly great way to test a service. Think about giving a small group of potential customers a discount in exchange for feedback.

SKILL FIVE – Being able to help others be more methodical and organised in their thinking

It is one thing for us to start to get better at standing back from our ideas and to be able to think them through, but can you encourage other people to do so as well? This is about being better at leading and working with others, which will start to affect the environment and culture in which you work. What can happen often, when trying to innovate, is that, if you are working in a group or team, each person may be thinking about different things and in different directions, misunderstanding each other and not really thinking through what they are trying to do. Edward de Bono, in his famous book *Six Thinking Hats*, talks of how to separate thinking into six clear functions or roles so that you can approach, from different angles, the complexities of a problem. Each Hat has a colour and a Purpose: White (discuss facts), Red (discuss feelings), Green (generate creativity), Yellow (design benefits), Black (investigate cautions) and Blue (follow process). This allows groups to orientate their thinking in a systematic way and, in so doing, to think together more effectively so as to produce better results. This form of lateral or parallel thinking can aid the development of ideas, allowing for a focused, systematic and coordinated approach.

TOOLS

Six Thinking Hats®

1 Do you naturally wear one of the Hats more than others?
   - How could you apply this way of thinking to your innovation challenge?

2 If you are a leader, or team manager, practise wearing the Blue Hat (process).
   - Facilitate others to think things through from the thinking directions of the different Hats.

3 If you do not consider yourself systematic, find someone you know who is.
   - Encourage them to ask questions to provoke and challenge you to think things through from different perspectives.

SKILL SIX – Being able to create an environment where people are encouraged to explore and question

When we are small children, asking questions is something that we all do very naturally. It is estimated that, at the age of 3, children ask 300 questions a day, no doubt infuriating their parents. It is no surprise that the decline in our ability to be creative coincides with the decline in our ability to ask questions. 'Stop asking so many questions,' a frustrated parent may say. 'This is the way to do something,' a manager may tell. As we grow older and busier, we have less and less time to stand back from what we are doing and ask ourselves, and others, questions.

Here are four tips to help create a culture of inquiry:

1 Encourage leaders and managers to ask 'what if?'
2 Within meetings, put on your agenda, 'What questions do we need to ask ourselves?' and create space for reflection.
3 Encourage and reward experimentation; build this into the INVESTIGATE phase as a way of working.
4 Teach people how to ask questions, and equip them with the tools, knowledge and time to practice and learn.

ACTIVITY

Ask good questions

There are many great books and approaches on how to get better at asking questions, some of which I have outlined in the Resource Guide at the end of this chapter.

1 This week, reframe, at least once a day, what you want to say to someone else into a question.

   You are banned from saying 'Have you tried this ...?' This is not a question of enquiry.

2 Use open-ended questions that will invite someone to open up and tell you about their situation and what they think.
3 Ring-fence some funding for yourself (or others) to test potential solutions with customers or to conduct experiments.
4 Set some time aside each month for yourself and others to get out of your, or their, normal day-to-day working routines and spend time out of the office talking to and listening to customers.

Dangers of Missing Out the *INVESTIGATE* Stage

- You (or your team) may have ideas but lack a clear value proposition (what is the benefit to someone and why would they buy or use it)?
- Ideas may not be workable or implementable.
- Ideas may be weak and lack rigour.
- Ideas generated may not be based on real customer or market insight.

THE INVESTIGATE MINDSET

'PAYING CAREFUL ATTENTION TO WHATEVER IS BEING STUDIED'

CRITICAL

'So, when you look at the data, what can you see?' I asked a group of commercial directors in a professional services organisation as I presented their team profile on The Six 'I's of Innovation®.

'It looks like we miss the *investigate* stage altogether,' replied one member of the team. 'We just jump headfirst into *implementation*.'

'Yes,' I responded, 'and why do you think that is the case?' 'Pressure for results,' said one. 'Activity is rewarded,' said another. 'No time to stop and think,' said a third.

'And what is the lowest attribute score in the team?' I asked. They stared at the graphs of their team results.

'Being able to make sure ideas are useful, not just novel,' one woman said. The others nodded in agreement.

'And what is the outcome of this on the quality of your products and services, and your sales?' I asked. There was a pause. It was as if, in seeing the data in front of them, a fresh wave of insight came into the room and they realised that they were not spending enough time with customers; not just to sell to them, but to explore where new needs were emerging and whether the solutions they had on offer were what customers really wanted. They were not getting outside of their own ways of thinking. They were not exploring or testing. Yes, they had ideas, but they were not thought through value propositions based on real customer or market insight.

This is a very, very common pattern in organisational life. Thankfully, in this case, the conversation sparked a discussion, and ideas, on how they could involve the customer in the heart of their innovation process, helping the team to create new solutions that directly met their customers' needs.

Being *critical* is often thought of as a negative behaviour, synonymous with being judgmental or accusatory. In fact, the word *critical* comes from *critique* and carries the sense of well-reasoned, articulate and in-depth examination of ideas or the quality of a something, not the thing itself. The essence, or mindset, that we want to develop is being objective, being able to stand outside of our own judgement so we can look through a microscope or a magnifying glass at what we have created and see how it could work. It is having the mindset of a researcher. This phase of innovation is about being informed, looking from different perspectives through deep analysis and assessment of what it is you are trying to create and being willing to test assumptions. You want to be the critic, a person who offers reasoned judgement. Critical thinking is an analytical skill, being thoughtful, asking questions, not taking things at face value and being willing to shift opinion as new information or insight comes to light.

This is not just about outsourcing to external research partners, although that may well be needed, depending on what it is that you want to create. This is about you, or your teams, spending time thinking through ideas you have so that you can develop them into propositions that will create value and have an impact. Do not outsource your eyes. Get out and meet customers, have the conversations, stand in their shoes and see what life is like from their perspective. Empathise with them and their needs. Think through the benefits that you can offer them and how can you deliver those benefits. Prototype, test, run small pilots or studies with small groups of people to see what might work, get feedback and enhance your offer. If you are using online technology, you have the benefit of being able to track how people are interacting with your service and gather instant feedback.

Think of ways you can explore and research that are appropriate to your innovation challenge and your cultural context. Many say they are scared to innovate because of the fear of failure. If you build in the requirement for failure at the *investigate* stage, people will know that it is OK to experiment, ask questions, explore and challenge. Articulating upfront that you expect many ideas to fail will save time, money and resources, because it is cheaper to fail during testing rather than to fail after full-scale *implementation*.

A useful question to ask yourself is 'What does the idea need?' It is not about you, it is about the success of the idea. The role of an innovator is to find out what the idea needs in order to move it forwards. Does it need more novelty? If so, go back to *ignite*. Does it need more testing? Go to *investigate*. Does it need resourcing? Go to *invest*. The skill, as you journey through The Six 'I's®, is to notice when you need to shift your or your team's thinking, particularly in the first three stages as you go back and forth between *identify*, *ignite* and *investigate*. At some point, though, you do need to make a decision, and this requires *courage*. This brings us to the fourth 'I' of The Six 'I's of Innovation®, which we will explore in the next chapter – *invest*.

Want to Develop a Critical Mindset?

An orientation and attitude that is willing to question, test assumptions and validate ideas in order to solve problems big and small.

TRY THIS

1 Build your empathy muscle. Theresa Wiseman, a medical scholar, attributes four skills that are common to people who are good at empathising:

- **Perspective taking** – the ability to take the perspective of another person
- **Staying out of judgement** – not easy to do, as our minds are often full of judgement and analysis

- **Recognising emotion in others** – being able to notice the subtle changes in how people feel
- **Communicating this to them** – the ability to acknowledge that you have heard someone, not necessarily offer them solutions for why they might be feeling the way they are

2 So, how do you do this?

- When you are next in conversation with someone, become the listener, rather than the talker. If you talk, ask questions, rather than give opinions. Refrain from wanting to tell your story or give your examples. Put the emphasis on listening to the other person.
- As you listen, see if you can hold yourself back from mentally making conclusions about what you are hearing. Stay in an open-minded framework. What language are they using? What is important to them? What are their values?
- Listen for the underlying emotion when someone speaks. Is it excitement, boredom, frustration, sadness, joy, despair, fear? Learn to listen for emotional content as much as you do facts or concepts.
- Use phrases such as 'um …', 'I see …', 'It sounds like you are …'. Keep soft eye contact and stay attentive to what they are saying to you without letting your mind wander somewhere else.

3 For becoming more systematic, try out these ideas:

- Predict what will happen tomorrow based on what happened today.
- Take an impulsive decision you have made and look at it rationally.
- Assemble a scale model following the instructions or buy a piece of furniture from IKEA and work out how to put it together.
- Make a personal budget and stick to it.
- Make a daily list and tick off all the items as you complete them.
- Arrange tools, cutlery and the contents in a cupboard in a neat and tidy way.
- Be 10 minutes early for all your appointments.
- Arrange your family or holiday photos into themed albums.
- Cook a meal and follow what the recipe says without changing anything.

If you make these *Critical* mindset activities part of your life you will build your capacity to think things through as well as develop a more empathetic style of communication.

Ready to move on to *invest*? Revisit your *Purpose*, at the beginning of the book, and use this simple checklist to make sure you have covered some of the most salient points of *investigate*. How have your ideas changed?

Activity	Complete
I have created selection criteria and assessed my ideas for their innovation impact.	
I have created a clear value proposition and communicated it to a potential customer and they see its relevance to their needs.	
I have investigated my ideas using an empathetic approach with potential customers.	
I have practised some left-brain activities to develop a more systematic approach.	

To dig deeper into developing the skills and mindset, refer to the resources at the end of this chapter, but first let us meet Jacquie Ford, whose highest score on The Six 'I's® is *investigate*.

LET'S MEET JACQUIE FORD

THE INVESTIGATOR PROFILE

Name:	Jacquie Ford
Job:	Business marketing, Global Campaigns
Company:	Facebook, Silicon Valley, USA
Primary Six 'I's® strength:	Investigator

What challenge are you looking to solve with innovation right now?

I work on implementing global marketing programmes. This is not new to large corporates, but it is new to Facebook. The role is complex as it involves harnessing the diversity of so many different stakeholders across the world with all their different needs and requirements. Although our initial campaign ideas may be considered innovative, the execution of them is multifaceted and requires good *investigate* and *implementation* skills to make the innovation work.

Looking at your Six 'I's® results, you are an *investigator*. How does this knowledge impact or change the way you work?

In Facebook, playing to our strengths is not new. What I liked about The Six 'I's® is it is specific to innovation strengths, and about how I contribute to making new ideas work. It has given me confidence in knowing that my core skills are fundamental to making things work. Without good *investigation*, we can waste time or not really understand the needs that we are trying to solve or our customer requirements. There are only so many hours in the day. Focusing on what I am good at, rather than trying to be good at everything, is what I try to do. This helps me to have more impact.

How do you play to your strengths? What advice would you give other people who want to get better at *investigate*?

It is about building relationships, listening and taking the time to hear the needs of different people. The more you can do this, the more you learn to put aside your own assumptions so you can understand whether an idea will work. This gives you more information and better information allows you to make more quality decisions. I work with many project managers and sometimes they just want to go head first into *implementation*. I encourage them to listen to others and see how they can solve problems, to be more agile and create space for testing and experimentation.

What steps, if any, would you take to improve the areas where you are not so strong or that are important to you and how?

I think it is three things. First, it is great to know your strengths and where you most naturally contribute and to build a role around these strengths. This builds confidence and makes you more impactful. Second, it is good to know where you are not as confident so that you can work with others who will complement you and, third, it gives you insight into where there may be opportunities to develop new skills. For example, I am lower on *invest* skills and would love to be more entrepreneurial in investing.

How has The Six 'I's® helped you and your teams/business? What examples, if any, can you share?

Thankfully, we have an entrepreneurial culture at Facebook. But, while we are encouraged to think differently and are working with innovative technology, we still have to build the skill to utilise and harness the diversity that we have. In rolling out global campaigns, we are using large-scale implementation processes to manage stakeholders across four regions. This is largely operational and needs excellent teamwork to deliver on the complexity. I am able to think consciously about how to put people together who have different strengths. The Six 'I's® is a great Model for building project teams.

Have you produced something you would consider innovative?

We *identified* a new opportunity, which we have named demotainment – demonstrating our products by actively using them in Facebook business to business marketing. Using lateral thinking, we *ignited* ideas that showcase our advertising platform and the benefits of our products by using them the same way our clients would. We are able, in real time, to *investigate* how they are working, due to the technology that we use, but it is more than that. We have had to challenge our ways of thinking – the traditional ways of doing advertising – to create powerful opportunities for our customers to innovate in how they advertise their products and services.

THE INVESTIGATE RESOURCE GUIDE

Here is a selection of resources for further exploration to get better at investigating ideas and developing a constructively critical mindset.

RESOURCE GUIDE

- Want to find out more about Design Thinking? Go to this great article on Forbes website for more information: www.forbes.com/sites/reuvencohen/2014/03/31/design-thinking-a-unified-framework-for-innovation/
- Learn from the experts in this 90-minute crash course in Design Thinking from Stanford University d.school: https://dschool.stanford.edu/dgift/
- Want to know more about the Three Horizons? Explore Paul Hobcraft's site, which has lots of great information and resources: www.agilityinnovation.com/index.php/unique-value-propositions/three-horizon-methodology
- Strategyzer's website is excellent for helping you to design a value proposition and business model: https://strategyzer.com
- This is a great resource for developing value propositions: https://conversionxl.com/value-proposition-examples-how-to-create/
- Some good examples of value propositions and why they work: www.wordstream.com/blog/ws/2016/04/27/value-proposition-examples

- Some inspiring examples of Design Thinking from Japan: https://econsultancy.com/blog/68443-13-inspiring-examples-of-design-thinking-from-japan/
- The story of Airbnb and how they used a Design Thinking approach: http://firstround.com/review/How-design-thinking-transformed-Airbnb-from-failing-startup-to-billion-dollar-business/
- What's your Inquiry Quotient? Try this short test at: http://amorebeautifulquestion.com/whats-your-inquiry-quotient-quiz/
- Have a browse of Warren Berger's site for useful content, insight and inspiration on questioning: http://amorebeautifulquestion.com

FURTHER READING

Great books on questioning

Berger, W. (2016) *A More Beautiful Question: The Power of Inquiry to Spark Breakthrough Ideas*. Bloomsbury USA.

Rothstein, D. and Santana, L. (2011) *Make Just One Change: Teach Students to Ask their Own Questions*. Harvard Education Press.

Schein, E. (2013) *Humble Enquiry: The Gentle Art of Asking Instead of Telling*. Berrett-Koehler Publishers.

Sobel, A. and Panas, J. (2012) *Power Questions*. John Wiley & Sons.

Stock, G. (2013) *The Book of Questions*. Workman Publishing.

Vogt, E. E., Brown, J. and Isaacs, D. (2003) *The Art of Powerful Questions, Catalysing Insight, Innovation and Action*. Whole System Associates.

Methodologies and tools

Baghai, M., Coley, S. and White, D. (2000) *The Alchemy of Growth: Practical Insights for Building the Enduring Enterprise*. Basic Books.

Brown, T. (2009) *Change by Design*. Harper Business.

de Bono, E. (2000) *Six Thinking Hats*. Penguin.

Mortee, I. (2013) *Design Thinking for Strategic Innovation: What They Can't Teach You at Business Or Design School*. John Wiley & Sons.

Osterwalder, A. and Pigneur, Y. (2010) *Business Model Generation: A Handbook for Visionaries, Game Changers and Challengers*. John Wiley & Sons.

Ries, E. (2011) *The Lean Startup: How Constant Innovation Creates Radically Successful Businesses*. Portfolio Penguin.

Smith, A., Osterwalder, A., Bernarda, G., Papadakos, T. and Pigneur, Y. (2014) *Value Proposition Design: How to Create Products and Services Customers Want*. John Wiley & Sons.

Stickdom, M. (2014) *This Is Service Design Thinking: Basics – Tools - Cases*. Bis Publishers.

Leadership and culture

Bungay Stanier, M. (2016) *The Coaching Habit: Say Less, Ask More & Change the Way You Lead Forever*. Box of Crayons Press.

Giudice, M. and Ireland, C. (2013) *Rise of the DEO: Leadership by Design (Voices That Matter)*. New Riders.

Tennant Snider, N. and Duarte, D. (2008) *Unleashing Innovation: How Whirlpool Transformed an Industry*. Wiley.

INVEST

HAVE COURAGE AND PERSUADE OTHERS TO BACK IDEAS

'That is great, we have a range of excellent propositions we can *investigate* further,' said a satisfied client after we had completed an innovation project that involved creating insights and propositions for a new product range. The propositions went into the *investigation* stage, through a number of qualitative focus groups and online testing, and some of them were improved. Others were put to one side, as, for one reason or another, they were not going to work. Then everything went quiet, very quiet. We found out, months later, that, while the business case was thorough and the organisation was able to deliver on creating the propositions, a decision in senior leadership just could not be made. There was hesitancy that that winning proposition was just too new; no one else was doing anything like it and there was fear about whether it would really work. Nothing happened.

The following year, a competitor launched a very similar product into the market and it was, and remains, a best seller. Our client had missed the opportunity.

This experience, and countless others that I have witnessed, made me realise, more than ever, that just generating new ideas and being creative is only half the story. People, and the decisions they make, culture and its propensity to support risk, or not, processes and whether they can enable ideas that may be Horizon 2 or 3, play a very, very large part in whether an idea will even get off the starting block. No matter how good it is.

It is one thing to have an idea, it is another to have *investigated* whether the idea may work, but it does not stop there. One needs to *invest*. To take action. One needs to have courage and to take a risk. This means walking into the unknown. You need to move from where you are, whether metaphorically or psychologically, and do something different. You do not know what will happen. You do not know if things will be a disaster or a failure, or an unbelievable success. It is rarely one or the other anyway. But to be able to say yes, I am going to have a go, requires a mindset of *courage*, as well as emotional and mental resilience and determination, and skills to get others to back your ideas. The need for this mindset and *invest* skills are the subject of this chapter.

The *invest* phase is central to innovation for, without firm commitment and courage, good ideas just remain good ideas. Amongst a raft of skills, *invest* requires the ability to assess and sanction detailed business plans, make pragmatic decisions under stressful conditions and judge where and when to allocate resources. Innovation requires saying 'no' as well as 'yes'. These are important skills, as innovation requires stopping ideas as well as backing them, as time, money and resources are often limited and difficult choices have to be made.

Getting timing right is extremely important too so you need to question your overall intent and *Purpose* of what you are trying to do. You need to ask yourself, is it the right time to make a decision and what decision needs to be made? Sometimes, in the case of the story I told, you do not know if timing is right, but a *courageous* decision may need to be made anyway.

The ability to influence is also a necessary skill set throughout the whole journey of innovation, but at the *invest* stage, one's ability to influence others to support an idea is critical. Influencing other organisations and people to create partnerships will also be required, so think through what support – whether it is time, money or expertise – you may need from other sources.

If you are in a position of leadership, you may need to train and develop others to communicate compelling reasons for why their ideas should be encouraged. This will help to develop an innovative culture, as enabling others to improve their ability to influence, backed by a strong case for investment, will ensure that more good ideas are supported, and innovation is not left to random chance. *Invest* is central to innovation, for without courage to make decisions and take action, good ideas will not transform into innovations.a

THE INVESTOR PROFILE

Innovation role – Providing pragmatism, decision making and influence
Mindset – Courage

Investor's strengths:

1. Being good at taking into account complex information and being able to make decisions
2. Understanding whether a business model might work
3. Being pragmatic under stressful conditions
4. Judging where and when to allocate time, money, people and resources
5. Influencing other organisations and people to create partnerships
6. Having the courage to take a risk

The image represents the mindset of ***Commitment****. The swirls start to form a shape. They converge in on themselves to direct energy into focused activity.*

Investor's challenges

Investors need a good combination of logical and pragmatic thinking, with a willingness to follow their hunches and take a risk. These are often difficult skills to combine. Some barriers can include:

- The need to ask for information that might be hard to quantify, which can slow down decision making
- Not allocating separate funds outside normal day-to-day business requirements
- Having too many conflicting demands on limited resources
- Failing to help others grow in their ability to influence and becoming a 'bottle neck' in making things happen

A challenge for *investors* is to improve their ability to sense whether timing is right, as a great idea at the wrong time may not have the desired impact.

HOW TO COMMUNICATE WITH *INVESTORS*

Depending on the combination of 'I's on someone's profile, here are a few do's and don'ts that will help you communicate more effectively with *investors*.

Do's	**Don'ts**
Be down to earth and pragmatic, be realistic with goals.	Over-inflate your assumptions or have unrealistic expectations.
Have a clearly articulated business plan and business model.	Rely on your creativity or enthusiasm at the expense of a good plan.
Demonstrate how your idea fulfils an unmet customer or market need.	Have a vague proposition that is not tested with potential users or customers.
Be courageous and bold. Communicate a clear plan of action on how you will minimise risk and make your proposition work.	Think you can do things alone. Show that you have the right people (or partnerships) to help you bring the proposition to life.

THE INVEST SKILLS

While there are many skills that help us to *invest* in ideas, we will focus on six core attributes critical to this phase of innovation:

1 To critically evaluate and make decisions on business plans
2 To keep cool and make decisions despite difficulties
3 To sense where and when resources should be provided
4 To be good at convincing others to collaborate
5 To be willing to step into the unknown despite challenges
6 To help others develop the skills of persuasion

Let us look at each one in turn.

Below is a top-line summary of the skills and their associated tools and activities for the area of *invest*.

Skills	Tools	Activities
To critically evaluate and make decisions on business plans	Business Model Canvas	Create a plan
To keep cool and make decisions despite difficulties		Portfolio Planning
To sense where and when resources should be provided	Decision evaluator	Assess your decisions
To be good at convincing others to collaborate		Develop partnerships
To be willing to step into the unknown despite challenges	Vision board	Scrutinise your business plan
To help others develop the skills of persuasion	Pitching	

SKILL ONE – Being able to critically evaluate and make decisions on business plans

Whether you have a complex proposition that needs comprehensive analysis with supporting evidence of a market opportunity or a smaller scale project or new business process, you are going to need some sort of plan. The detail and depth of your plan will depend on what you are trying to do but, regardless of the scale, developing the ability to create, assess and, where appropriate, sanction a plan, is a core *invest* skill. What you are trying to do is understand if there is proof of market (POM). The *investigate* phase is concerned more with proof of concept (POC) – is the value proposition addressing a real need? The *invest* stage is taking it a step further, what is the size of market opportunity, does your business model work and can you deliver on the plan? Even if you are in an entrepreneurial venture, where a plan may have to be more flexible, you still need a plan. At least you are aware that it is changing, rather than blindly moving forward into *implementation* without a clear idea of what you are doing and how you are planning to make it work. And do not leave it to hope. Hope is not a strategy.

ACTIVITY

Create a plan

So, what are you looking for in a good plan? There are many things, but these are the most important.

1. Firstly, there needs to be a well-thought through *value proposition*, not just an idea but a validated proposition that addresses a need. If not, go back to *investigate* and make sure you have one.
   - If it is a commercial innovation that you are creating, how are you going to make money?
   - What is your business model? How are you going to price your service offering?
   - If you do not think you will break even until year three, how are you going to fund three years of business activity with no revenue?

   You might have a great value proposition but, if no one is going to buy it, or *invest* in it, then it might not be a good business opportunity.
2. Secondly, *who are your customers*, how are you going to reach or attract them to you?
   - What is your marketing strategy?
   - What volume of sales do you anticipate will come through each channel or route to market?

3 And, lastly, and some say most importantly, *who is going to do what*? Who is on the team?

- Whether inside a company, or outside, whether a group of employees or networks of colleagues, or advisors, do you have the skill to deliver the proposition to your customers?

TOOLS

Business Model Canvas

One excellent tool for thinking through aspects of how your idea might work is the Business Model Canvas, created by Strategyzer. More information on how to use the Canvas is in the resource guide at the end of this chapter.

Source: https://strategyzer.com/canvas/business-model-canvas

SKILL TWO – Being able to keep cool and make decisions despite difficulties

Cool, objective, dispassionate – qualities that are important in making decisions under stress. Innovating can be a stressful endeavour, largely because you are treading on unfamiliar territory. You are trying something new. Even if you are not putting your personal money into something, you still need to make choices about time, resources and other forms of investment material. This requires a particular type of pragmatism. The ability to evaluate decisions with the facts that you have, as well as discern, with your gut instinct, whether you should act or not is a curious combination. At this stage of innovation, many ideas stop. Even good ones. Even those that have been developed using a robust innovation process. The *investigate* phase may have proven that there is desire for what you want to develop but, unless you can get support for it, amidst the stress of other demands being made on time and funds, the idea can end up collecting dust on the shelf. In corporate life, one of the biggest reasons we have observed is the lack of funding focused on innovative initiatives outside of business as usual (BAU) or core business activity (Horizon 1). There can be great excitement at training people to generate ideas, creating innovation teams, getting people to be more customer-focused, but, if you cannot support the outcomes of this training or coaching, then both the enthusiasm of people, plus the potential of new ideas, is not embedded or reinforced in the organisational culture.

ACTIVITY

Portfolio planning

1 Whether you are working in an organisation or for yourself, set aside some time and money that is purely for investing in doing something new.
2 Think like an investor:

- Take a portfolio approach to the decisions you make. We know that of all the ventures and ideas that are started, there are a lot that do not succeed, so expect that some ideas are not going to work.
- Hedge your bets; make decisions on some that have a higher risk and others that do not.

SKILL THREE – Being able to sense where and when resources should be provided

As part of our work, we coach managers on how they can drive innovation in their workplace. Some are corporate, some are more entrepreneurial, and they have very different challenges.

Here are two such examples:

David is a Chinese manager in a large multinational based in Shanghai. He has limited time, and budget, to allocate to projects that are not about day-to-day operational issues (Horizon 1), but he knows that, if the business focuses only on what is important in the short term, it will miss out on new growth opportunities (Horizon 2) and bigger, more disruptive innovation opportunities (Horizon 3). He also wants to encourage his team to think differently and create improvements in their day-to-day operational projects.

Samantha is a Singaporean entrepreneur who has left her corporate job to set up her own business. From having a range of support available in her former organisation, she now realises she has to become a master at many things she formerly knew nothing about. How much time should she spend meeting potential clients? What about developing her website and social media strategy? When is she going to have the time to spend improving her product and working with suppliers?

Both David and Samantha have to make a judgement call about where and when to allocate resources. For David, it is not just about money, but coaching support and management. For Samantha, it is about where and when to allocate her most limited resource: time.

ACTIVITY

Assess your decisions

Think over the last week about the investment decisions you have made with the resources that you currently have.

1 Reflect back on your *Purpose* statement. What has been the impact of those decisions on what you are trying to do? High, medium or low?

2 What do you need to do differently?

3 Become more conscious of how you are using your time:

- Are you just busy, but not really focused on outcomes?
- How can you change this?

TOOLS

Decision evaluator

1 Draw up a grid with four boxes. On one axis, write *Potential benefits*, on the other write *Potential costs*, both with high and low at each end of the scale.

- Think through your value proposition(s) and place them onto the grid in the relevant box.

- What insight does this give you?

Potential costs		
	High **Forget it**	**High** **Explore it**
	Enhance it **Low**	**Do it** **High**

Potential benefits

2 Go back to your business plan.
   - What is your budget?
   - Where do you need to allocate resources?
   - Create a cash flow projection of what you will need to spend versus where your anticipated revenue will come from and when.
   - What decisions might you need to make about how you allocate the resources that you have? Cash is king.

Investor Warren Buffet says part of making good investment decisions is to look at the bad ones you have made and work out why they did not work. What can you learn about bad investment decisions you have made in the past?

DID YOU KNOW?

Designer, inventor and multibillionaire James Dyson *identified* an opportunity for innovation when he noticed that even the most powerful vacuum cleaner pushed dirt around the room, rather than sucking it up. He *ignited* an idea after looking at the mechanics of industrial sawmills, which used cyclonic separators to remove dust from the air. He became curious about how the principle of separation might work on a vacuum cleaner. After rigging up a prototype, he realised it worked. Dyson spent five years *investigating* and refining his ideas by making and testing prototypes, while his wife supported him financially as an Art teacher. Five thousand, one hundred and twenty-seven prototypes failed. Most people thought Dyson was mad. He showed his prototype to domestic appliance manufacturers who did not want it, so decided to *invest* in the idea himself by borrowing $900,000 with his house as security on the loan. Gradually, he started to sell his idea into catalogues, but his big break came when, through his personal network, he started to sell through a large retailing outlet in the UK in 1995.

Dyson's 58 products generated $2.4 billion in sales in 2016 and an estimated $340 million in net profits, even after 46 per cent of the company's EBITDA (earnings before interest, taxation, depreciation and amortisation) was reinvested in research and development, more than competitors.

Source: www.forbes.com/sites/chloesorvino/2016/08/24/james-dyson-exclusive-top-secret-reinvention-factory/#4f72bd3d2e87

Dyson's story, while quite well-known in the UK, illustrates just how tough it can be to raise capital to *invest* in an innovative solution and take it to market. No doubt, this type of story can be replicated many times across many different examples and countries. He *identified* an area of opportunity; he *ignited* a solution to the problem that he saw. He *investigated* it through prototyping and testing – 5,127 prototypes – he *invested* his own time and money but, actually, it was not until he leveraged his networks and connections that his big break came. This shows how important a multitude of skills are, and the connections we have, when it comes to innovation, also serendipity and being in the right place at the right time. What you want to do is increase your chances of success by optimising your skill set *and* positioning yourself where lucky breaks can happen for you, too. Control what you can, but do not underestimate the power of synchronicity.

SKILL FOUR – Being able to be good at convincing others to collaborate

When my husband and I moved to Singapore in 2010, we engaged the United Kingdom Trade and Industry (UKTI) to help us set up meetings with potential clients. If we did not have that partnership, we probably would not have been successful getting started. We were clear on who our customers were and what we offered, but we needed help to access the right decision makers. The UKTI knew the right people that we should talk to, and could access them through the relationships that they had with companies in Singapore. If we had just gone door knocking, I am not sure we would have had the same response. It certainly would have taken us a lot longer to build the business.

If you are going to make a success of what you want to do, in innovation more than in other aspects of work, you need to think through what partnerships will accelerate market access. Depending on the nature and scale of what you are doing, there may be a range of partnerships that you will need. Marketing, sales, technological development, legal, intellectual property, finance, design, to name just a few. Your ability to influence others is a critical skill, if you are going to get off the runway and start to fly.

ACTIVITY

Create partnerships

1 Look at your plan.

- What skills and experience are you lacking?
- Who do you need to help you deliver it?
- Make a list of the expertise that you will need.
- Think of people in your network, or people in the network of those you know. Are there people who can help or do they know of others?

Remember the skill of expanding your networks from the *identify* chapter.

It will help here, too.

2 If you are developing something that has an intellectual property (IP) element and you are not in a large organisation, find yourself a good IP lawyer and legal advice that can protect what you are developing.

3 Become a storyteller.

- Craft your propositions into compelling stories that open people's hearts and minds. Check out the resource guide at the end of this chapter for ideas on how. This will help to develop charisma and enthuse others to back your ideas.

SKILL FIVE – Being able to be willing to step into the unknown despite challenges

'How can senior executives promote value innovation? First, they must identify and articulate the company's prevailing logic. Then they must challenge it,' say authors, W. Chan Kim and Renée Mauborgne in their international bestseller, *Blue Ocean Strategy*. This takes courage. *Courage* requires risk. If there is no risk of loss, then one does not need *courage*. If you are going to challenge the prevailing logic of how an industry or company works, and the competitive dynamics in which it operates, then you are going to have to go against what is perceived as normal, given and safe. For example, who thought Apple would become a music and entertainment platform (iTunes) or that flying would become ubiquitous for ordinary people (AirAsia, easyJet)? Flying was a premium-priced experience for wealthy tourists or business travellers. Not so any more and, even those markets, and many others, are changing dramatically. To have *courage*, one has to have faith and vision. You need to see in your mind's eye the outcome of what you want to create. This is needed at the *invest* stage. To innovate is a creative act, but the act of creation is more than getting an idea; it requires *courageous* action to drive momentum and energetically move an idea into existence.

TOOLS

Vision board

Revisit your *Purpose*.

1 Create a vision board of what you want to create. Make it as colourful and impactful as you can. You can choose images from the web or cut images out of magazines.

2 Imprint these images into your imagination or imagine you were reading an article about what you had created:

- What magazine would publish your story?
- What would be the headline?
- Write it up and read it until it feels believable and energises you with renewed vision and *courage*.

Scrutinise your business plan

Find someone you trust that can scrutinise your business plan and challenge your thinking. You may or may not decide to go ahead, but at least you will make a decision with your eyes wide open having thought through the potential risks.

Courage is not just about saying *yes*. You cannot do everything and you have to focus. Say *no* to something that might distract you from your goal.

SKILL SIX – Being able to help others develop the skills of persuasion

I had the opportunity, a few years ago, of studying with one of the world's foremost thinkers in the field of group dynamics and non-verbal communication, Michael Grinder. For 10 months, we learnt how to increase our range of non-verbal influencing and communication skills and each week we had to submit an assignment about how we were incorporating the skills into our daily lives. Grinder says, 'Influence happens in the mind of someone else.' Think about that for a moment. If influence happens in the mind of someone else, our ability to see their perspective – of why they should back our proposition – is a very important skill to develop. In our work, we train and coach as much in the ability to influence as we do in how to be creative and generate new ideas. If you want to develop a culture of innovation, it is not just about your personal ability to influence, but whether you can help others do the same. Time and time again, ideas, often good ones, stop at this phase of the innovation journey. People may well have great ideas, but because they lack the ability to influence other decision makers they do not get visibility or support. It is often the loudest voice or the person with the most political influence that will be heard. If ideas can come from anywhere, this is not a great recipe for innovation.

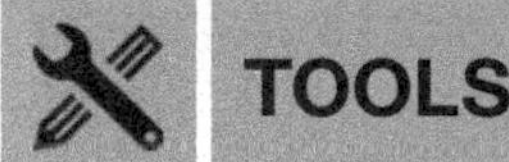

TOOLS

Develop a pitch

1 Imagine you had one minute to convince someone to buy what you have created.
   - What would you say?
   - Practise writing up a script and try it out on a few people.
   - What is their reaction?
   - Teach someone else to do the same.
2 Present your solution to someone who thinks very differently from you.
   - Do they understand it?
   - If not, how can you simplify your language and make it more compelling?
3 If you are a manager or leader of teams:
   - Schedule time for people to practise 'pitching' their ideas to each other;
   - Hire a professional to help teach your team pitching and influencing skills.

Here are key areas you need to include in your pitch:

1. Opening introduction – what is the value proposition?
2. Business model
3. Market/scalability
4. Competition/alternatives
5. Team
6. Projection (potential ROI benefits)
7. Current status (where are you now)?
8. Plan/timeline/budget required
9. Risks/contingencies
10. Closing story (value proposition)

Dangers of Missing Out the *INVEST* Stage

- You (or your team) might have unrealistic expectations of what will make the proposition work.
- You may not have a clearly thought-through business model.
- You are unable to influence anyone to support you in making the proposition real.
- You cannot get traction to take action.

THE INVEST MINDSET

'AN ATTITUDE THAT SPURS SOMEONE TO ACT DESPITE CHALLENGES OR DIFFICULTIES'

COURAGEOUS

Browsing through the British Airways *High Life* magazine on a long-haul flight from Singapore to the UK, a story caught my eye. It was the tale of Heston Blumenthal, innovator in food science and gastronomy, and his journey from self-taught cook to celebrity chef and owner of the Fat Duck, a three-starred Michelin Restaurant in England. A piece of dialogue stuck in my mind. 'So, what do you think of people when they call you a pioneer?' asked the journalist. 'Well, it is very easy to be called a pioneer by others when you have succeeded, as here I am telling you my story. If I had failed, people would have called me a loser,' he replied.

This is so true when we talk about risk and failure – often two elements we encounter when we try something new. We all love a rag-to-riches story. It is probably hard-wired into our minds. Through hard times and against the odds the person succeeded. There was a happy ending. In reality, though, we know that nine out of ten ventures do not make it. We do not read about those entrepreneurs or business people that re-mortgaged their houses, got into personal debt, lost everything for the belief in their idea, because they have no documented stories, unless they succeeded. Or, if we do know about them, we say, 'Poor John, he risked so much, did you know he lost his house? I knew it was never going to work.'

Doing new things creates stress. Period. Both inside your own psychology, but also in the social environment in which you live and work. The brain is learning, adapting and changing in response to new stimulus and experience. Culturally, there is pressure for immediate results, or to conform to what is seen as the right way of doing something, because that is the way it has always been done. To be a good innovator, one has to learn to see through this and have the courage, and confidence, to take action, even though you do not know exactly what the outcome will be.

More and more organisations want to encourage entrepreneurship, or at least an entrepreneurial mindset in their employees. If they are to do this, there needs to be a way for people to know that they can lose, they can even fail, but they will still be appreciated and valued. The organisation needs to build in this tolerance for experimentation and know that some of the choices or decisions that are made will not work, and that employees can face their own fear and act anyway. It is no good just talking about this. It has to move from head to heart. Many of us live privileged and relatively sheltered lives. Yes, some things may not be going the way we want them to or we have a curiosity about doing something new, but, most likely, we do not face these challenges on a daily basis and have some form of security to fall back on. We have homes to go to at night. We earn a regular income. So, how do we get to feel the edge of our own fear?

A few years back, we ran an innovation workshop for a group of managers from eight different countries across Asia. After discussing with our client, we decided to hold the session in Macau. When it came to talking about risk and fear, instead of just having an intellectual discussion about the need to take a risk, we took the whole team to the top of Macau Tower. At 233 metres, the Macau Tower's bungee jump from the outer rim is the highest commercial SkyJump in the world. The choice was to jump, do a skywalk around the perimeter's edge or climb to the top. You can imagine how rich the debrief was afterwards, when we got back to the workshop venue. It was not just an intellectual discussion any more. People had felt fear in their bodies and their minds and then they had taken action. For some, it was quite a revelation and they were proud that they had done something they had never done before.

Success is rarely in a straight line. The Six 'I's® is not a linear innovation Model. It is a journey. There are dead ends. There are disasters. There are small victories and, sometimes, for all manner of reasons, things can come together and work out. If you are to innovate, you need to develop this mindset of courage, or to face danger, difficulty or pain and act anyway. To notice your fear and to make a choice to try something new. It is not necessarily about having blind faith, not calculating or minimising the chance of failure, but the mindset of courage requires a step out into the unknown, and this is why a lot of people and organisations find it difficult to innovate.

I was a speaker at Caterpillar's Women's Initiative in Singapore a few years ago, and one woman asked me how she could be more courageous. It is an interesting question. If you find it natural to step out into the unknown, it is sometimes hard to explain how to do this to someone else. I answered her by saying, 'Do you feel just slightly uncomfortable about trying something new or saying something in a room full of people? You can feel your heart fluttering and your stomach churning, but then you say or do it? That is an act of courage. Start with small steps.'

Look at your innovation challenge. If you have *investigated* it well, you will have reduced risk, but there will still be an element of uncertainty. There has to be, otherwise it is business as usual. How else can you practise courage? So, you have made a decision to go forward or not. Then the fun really starts. You have to take your proposition and start to build it. You have to bring it forth into the world. This brings us to the fifth 'I' of The Six 'I's of Innovation®, which we will explore in the next chapter – *implement* and the mindset of *commitment*.

Want to Develop a *COURAGEOUS* Mindset?

An attitude that spurs someone to act despite challenges or difficulties.

TRY THIS

1 Feel through the fear
   - Notice how fear feels inside of you. Where does it sit? In your stomach, in your mind, in your chest? Become more familiar with the feeling and notice what triggers the emotion.
   - See fear like a big wave. Imagine you are surfing the wave on a surf board and have strength and confidence. Even if you get knocked off the board, you can get back on. See yourself going safely into the shore.
   - When you are next in a meeting and want to say something, but are worried about what people might think of you, say it anyway. Notice how you feel afterwards.
   - Put some music on that you like to dance to in the privacy of your home. Dance. Let go of self-consciousness.
   - Go out to a party and be the first to get on the dance floor. Dance as if no one is looking.
   - Make a list of five things you would really like to do, but are too scared to try. Make a resolution to try one of them out.

2 Give yourself an ambitious goal that you know will stretch you out of your comfort zone and challenge your thinking. Create a plan and start.

3 Develop a reflective practice. Choose what works for you.
   - Maybe it is long walks, sitting meditation, deep breathing or Qi Gong.
   - Learn to still the mind, away from the busyness of work; this will help you to have a clearer focus while you are working and to make better decisions.

Make these *courageous* mindset activities part of your life.

Ready to move on to *implement*? Revisit your *Purpose* statement and use this simple checklist to make sure you have covered some of the most salient points of *invest*. Do you need to go back to *ignite* or *investigate*? How strong is your proposition?

Activity	Complete
I have developed a plan around a clear customer value proposition and business model and have identified partnerships that can help make it work.	
I have assessed my proposition and understand resource implications and cost against benefits. I have raised some investment.	
I have created a vision board that motivates me and makes me feel courageous and inspired. I have practised moving through fear into courage.	
I have developed a pitch and communicated it to someone who can help me move the proposition forward.	

To dig deeper into developing the skill and mindset, refer to the resource guide at the end of this chapter, but first let us meet Thomas Nyegaard, whose highest score on The Six 'I's® is *invest*.

LET'S MEET THOMAS NYEGAARD

THE *INVESTOR* PROFILE

Name:	Thomas Nyegaard
Job:	Entrepreneur and Investor
Company:	Tradeworks
Primary Six 'I's® strength:	Investor

What challenge are you looking to solve with innovation right now?

I am an investment banker by background and worked in London for 13 years in institutional fixed income sales, serving Nordic clients and select hedge funds in London and New York. I started investing in startups as early as 2002 and, by 2009, I decided to move back to Copenhagen to join a small investment boutique in order to get more experience in investing in early-stage companies. I quickly realised that, in order to be a good investor, you have to have your own experience as an entrepreneur and this led me moving to Asia where I co-founded a startup called Tradeworks. Based in Singapore and Denmark, we enable retail traders to easily design and deploy automated trading strategies without any need for coding. It is a niche market that has been devoid of innovation for years. The challenge is to disrupt a manual, labour-intensive process through simplification and automation, where a machine can execute strategies. This helps to minimise the human risk that is normally associated with this type of trading.

Looking at your Six 'I's® results, you're an *investor*. How does this knowledge impact or change the way you work?

To be successful at innovation requires a combination of variables but, ultimately, you can't execute an idea without money. As an investor, I am always thinking what are my chances of a return on investment? Part of my responsibility in Tradeworks, as well as business development, is to raise finance for the company. Being an angel investor myself, I have a good understanding of what investors look for and how to get investor pitch decks right. This is always a much harder and time-consuming task than entrepreneurs expect while they have dozens of similarly important tasks to juggle as well. Sticking to realistic business plans, conservative budgets and common sense is key!

How do you play to your strengths? What advice would you give other people who want to get better at *investing*?

Most business plans fail because they are built on a dream. Only 5–10 per cent survive. When I look at a pitch deck, I water down everything I see. An entrepreneur is enthusiastic but their assumptions are often wrong. I look critically at the assumptions. I then take off 50 per cent of what the plan says and see if the business model will still make sense. Anyone can put in an excel spreadsheet with financial projections; the important thing is: can the entrepreneur adequately substantiate the numbers? Keep your feet on the ground. Be realistic. Things never turn out as you think. They take more time. They cost more money.

What steps, if any, would you take to improve the areas where you are not so strong or that are important to you and how?

It's important to bear in mind that when one leaves the corporate world to become an entrepreneur, all the resources that one might be used to will also be left behind. You need to do sales, you need to do business development, you need to keep finances in check and you risk ending up doing too much and not doing anything very well. I try to follow the Pareto rule where 80 per cent of the value is generated by focusing on 20 per cent of the tasks at hand. You have to be critical about what you need to do. I talk with my team about our strategic key performance indicators (KPIs) in order to identify exactly what needs to get done to generate most value and then we stick with it. It is often tempting to throw yourself off course with different opportunities that will invariably pop up. I try, as well, to keep inspired by meeting people in my industry who are doing innovative things who can challenge my thinking.

How has The Six 'I's® helped you and your teams/business? What examples, if any, can you share?

I believe that one of the biggest pitfalls in innovation and entrepreneurship is to have a hunch and just go with it. This is very dangerous. Just because you think you have a good idea and like it, or your friends like it, does not mean there is a market for what you want to create or do. The Six 'I's® helps to give a process so you do not miss out big steps; like investigating whether the idea will work, testing your assumptions, finding customers, getting the right stakeholders on board, building a value proposition that has a business model to support it. The rest is hard work and large doses of luck.

Have you produced something you would consider innovative?

Disrupting the market of foreign exchange is an innovative endeavour. *Identifying* the opportunity to simplify what is a complex and time-consuming activity and *igniting* ideas for automated software development was just the start. Now it is all about building the business and creating a sustainable financial platform for growth. *Investment*, *implementation* and continuous *improvement* are key going forward. Creating a sophisticated technology, enabled by a world-class user experience, is the vision and that keeps us going.

THE INVEST RESOURCE GUIDE

This section outlines some resources for further exploration to get better at *investing* in ideas and developing the mindset of *courage*.

RESOURCE GUIDE

ENTREPRENEURSHIP, INVESTING AND INFLUENCE

There are many sites, books and gurus who can help you become more entrepreneurial and influential. Below are just a few ideas to get you going.

- Here are two good articles – one on how to write a business plan: www.entrepreneur.com/article/247575; and another on how to pitch to investors: www.entrepreneur.com/article/251311
- Learn how to build your own Business Model Canvas: https://strategyzer.com/canvas/business-model-canvas
- Jennifer Lee, author of *The Right-Brain Business Plan*, has some great resources on her site for creative entrepreneurs or people who do not consider themselves natural business planners: www.rightbrainbusinessplan.com
- Learn from investor and entrepreneur Guy Kawasaki in 'The Essential Guide to Entrepreneurship': www.udemy.com/entrepreneurship-course-by-guy-kawasaki/
- In my opinion, the best trainer on non-verbal communication and group dynamics in the world is Michael Grinder. Learn about his work here: www.michaelgrinder.com

HANDLING STRESS

- Research shows that people spend almost 47 per cent of their waking hours thinking about something other than what they are doing. This can impair creativity and performance. Want to find out how mindful you are? Try this quiz: https://hbr.org/2017/03/assessment-how-mindful-are-you.
- Sign up to the Potential Project, a global company that brings mindfulness to organisations and leaders. Lots of tips, exercises and useful research into the importance of being mindful at work: www.potentialproject.com.
- Need guidance to help you practice mindfulness? Explore the work of Jon Kabat-Zinn, scientist, writer and meditation teacher who has brought mindfulness into the mainstream of medicine and society: www.mindfulnesscds.com.

DEVELOPING COURAGE

There is a lot we can learn about courage from outside the business world. Here are two quite different perspectives.

- Sammy Franco, one of the most recognised authorities on reality-based self-defence instruction and an innovator in martial arts, can teach you how to develop mental toughness in his book, *The 10 Best Mental Toughness Techniques* (2016, Contemporary Fighting Arts, LLC).
- Dr Robert Biswas-Diener, widely known as the Indiana Jones of Positive Psychology, will take you on a whirlwind journey about bravery in his book, *The Courage Quotient: How Science Can Make You Braver* (2012, Jossey Bass).

FURTHER READING

The following books are some of my favourites on influencing and storytelling, fundamental skills required to get backing for new ideas.

Barnes, K. (2015) *A Model for Exercising Influence: Building Relationships and Getting Results.* Published online: http://onlinelibrary.wiley.com/doi/10.1002/9781119158523.ch3/summary.

Berger, J. (2013) *Contagious: Why Things Catch on*. Simon & Schuster.

Callahan, S. (2016) *Putting Stories to Work: Mastering Business Story Telling*. Pepperberg Press.

Carnegie, D. (2006) *How to Win Friends and Influence People*. Vermilion.

Cialdini, R.B. (2017) *Influence: The Psychology of Persuasion*. CreateSpace Independent Publishing Platform.

Heath, C. and Heath, D. (2007) *Made to Stick: Why Some Ideas Survive and Others Die*. Random House.

Kawasaki, G. (2011) *Enchantment: The Art of Changing Hearts, Minds, and Actions*. Portfolio.

Pink, D.H. (2014) *To Sell Is Human: The Surprising Truth About Moving Others*. Canongate Books Ltd.

Schwartz, B. (2005) *The Paradox of Choice: Why More Is Less*. Harper Perennial.

IMPLEMENT

MAKE AN IDEA HAPPEN AND CREATE VALUE FROM IT

'Where are we going to find someone with that type of expertise?' I asked my colleague, as we discussed a new business idea. It was February 2000 and I had left a steady job, in a large organisation, to work in a corporate incubator – a department that focused solely on developing innovative businesses – in Hamburg in Germany. I was called a 'future shaper' – tasked with identifying new growth opportunities and developing propositions.

The buzz was electric, working day and night, as a small team of thinkers. We crystallised our ideas and sized the potential market for our new product.

'I know,' said one of the team. 'I have a friend who is a leading researcher into our area. He is the man.' So began our quest and deep dive into the world of psychology, as we created a partnership with Dr Gilles Spony, award-winning cross-cultural psychologist, to translate his 10-year research findings into an online assessment tool that could be used in organisational life.

After deliberation, it was decided that we needed to develop a partnership with a company that specialised in placing consultants and project managers into multinational companies. A couple of us, in the corporate incubator, were asked if we wanted to pioneer the new venture into the market. We did. What followed was two years of building, from scratch, a technology business that specialised in human capital development. My colleague taught himself to code and built the initial prototypes while we searched for an IT partner who could develop and help to scale the applications. I focused on business and product development, working closely with Dr Spony to create the service offering.

What we had not anticipated, however, despite the innovative application we had invented, was the conservative nature of buyers and the difficulty of bringing to market an innovative product. Eventually, we had successes with large business schools and a range of multinationals. However, *implementation* was difficult.

Herein lies a lesson for all of us. We may have *identified* an opportunity; in our case, the need for a leadership profile that could assess cultural differences. We have *ignited* a solution – for us, an online suite of applications that could measure individual, team and organisational values and the impact national culture had on leadership decisions. We may have raised some *investment* and built partnerships, but then the hard work really begins. *Implementation*. Often, we do not think of our ability to *implement* as part of being innovative, but it is. Without *implementation*, no innovation happens.

There are so many variables that make something work, particularly something innovative. As I look back on that time of my life, it is easy, with hindsight, to take it apart and scrutinise the mechanics as if it were a machine full of logic and formula. What is clear, though, is that innovating is hard work and requires discipline and determination to keep going, even when things get tough. Having an idea and a vision is essential, but not enough. This is the stage when we hit the wall of disappointment. We also have to know when we need to move on and let things go. This is also incredibly difficult to do, especially when you have invested so much personal energy into trying to make something succeed.

Our ability to *implement*, so we can see an idea come to fruition, is the subject for this chapter.

Throughout, I will give examples, tips and activities to help you improve your ability and confidence to *implement* new ideas.

This phase is central to innovation for, without the ability to take an idea through to *implementation*, value is not created and innovation does not happen. *Implementation* involves systematically completing tasks, planning and organising and managing risks. This is the hard work of innovation, as the ability to execute on a plan and get things done is paramount. The mindset for *implement* is being *committed*, seeing things through and making things happen.

Managing risk is important, too, as being able to scan the horizon and see where there might be potential problems can save a lot of time and money in the long run. From a leadership perspective, keeping people motivated to deliver on time and to budget and building the right team with the necessary skills are important behaviours. *Implementation* requires the ability to create and build strong teams with diverse experiences and competences.

Being able to motivate others can also help to drive productivity and efficiency and create a culture of innovation where people feel motivated to succeed. Sometimes, the competences or capabilities to execute on an idea may be lacking, so building alliances with other people and organisations could be critical. Partnering and collaborating is becoming increasingly important, so be mindful of this, as you might need to find potential partners in order to implement your ideas.

THE IMPLEMENTER PROFILE

Innovation role – Providing management, focus and discipline
Mindset – Commitment

Implementer's strengths:

1. Being good at planning and organising
2. Making things happen
3. Managing risks
4. Motivating others to achieve results
5. Building alliances and partnerships
6. Allocating and managing resources
7. Building and managing strong teams

The image represents the mindset of ***Commitment****. The swirls start to form a shape, they converge in on themselves to direct energy into focused activity.*

Implementer's challenges

Implementers like to get things done, and tend to be practical and focused, and action orientated but they can:

- Sometimes jump into action too quickly.
- Not allow time for investigating the feasibility of an idea.
- Lose sight of the innovative aspect of what they are trying to achieve.
- Get caught up in operational issues and stop focusing on the bigger picture.

Implementers tend to be action-orientated and pragmatic in their outlook. This may lead them to make decisions based more on practical feasibility rather than exploring creative alternatives that could help to ensure the novelty of an idea stays alive during the implementation process.

HOW TO COMMUNICATE WITH *IMPLEMENTERS*

Depending on the combination of 'I's on someone's profile, here are a few do's and don'ts that will help you communicate more effectively with *implementers*.

Do's	**Don'ts**
Be action-orientated and focused on results. Stick to deadlines.	Jump into a new activity without finishing what you are working on first.
Have a realistic plan, but communicate the need to deviate as circumstances change.	Continuously change your mind without involving them in decisions and getting their buy-in.
Involve them in building teams and partnerships.	Have vague targets, KPIs (key performance indicators) or leave things to chance.
Stay the course, remain committed, despite any setbacks.	Lack focus on core activities that need to be achieved.

THE IMPLEMENT SKILLS

While there are many skills that help us to *implement* ideas, we will focus on six core attributes critical to this stage of innovation:

1 To work out what needs to be done
2 To see responsibilities through to completion
3 To see what could go wrong and know how to minimise risk
4 To collaborate and build partnerships with others
5 To assemble teams with complementary skills and knowledge
6 To help people complete their work in allocated budgets and timeframes

Let us look at each one in turn.

Below is a top-line summary of the skills and their associated tools and activities for the area of *implement*.

Skills	Tools	Activities
To work out what needs to be done	Project planning Task allocation	Create a project plan
To see responsibilities through to completion		Decide on priorities Spend time with an implementer
To see what could go wrong and know how to minimise risk	Risk management	Create a board of advisors
To collaborate and build partnerships with others	Skills assessment	
To assemble teams with complementary skills and knowledge	Ways of working	Team dynamics Team vision board
To help people complete their work in allocated budgets and timeframes	Six 'I's® Tracker	Fit role to motivation

SKILL ONE – Being able to work out what needs to be done

Whether you are an entrepreneur, small business owner or working in a large organisation, we all have the same amount of time: 24 hours a day.

For most of us, we spend the majority of our days 'working', doing activities that generate income or keep us employed. We are busy. But, are we productive? Productivity is not about the number of hours that you work. It is about how smart you are with the time that you have to accomplish the results that you need to achieve. It is very tempting to spend a lot of time doing things so we look busy or have a feeling that we are moving towards a goal, but stand back and reflect on how you are spending your time. How much time are you sitting in meetings wishing you were somewhere else, or distracting yourself from doing something that should be higher on your list of priorities? The ability to plan and organise is a critical skill when trying to bring something new into the world. It is not planning for planning's sake; it is thinking through carefully what needs to be done that will help an idea get traction. Often, particularly in the early days of *implementing* something new, time is of the essence and cannot be wasted.

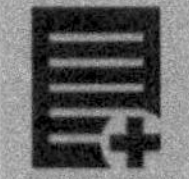

ACTIVITY

Create a project plan

Revisit your Purpose Statement.

1 When do you want to see your idea working and creating value?
2 Work back through The Six 'I's® to help you create a timeline and put in dates.
3 If you need to see results by a certain time, make sure you create space to focus on the first few 'I's so that you can make the solution more robust.
4 Keep yourself and others focused on the outcome of what you are trying to create.

Task allocation

Go back to your vision board from the *invest* stage. What will help you achieve your vision?

1 List all the things that need to be accomplished.
2 Categorise these into the following themes:
   - **Process** (operational and administrative)
   - **Change** (product and service development)
   - **Results** (sales, marketing and business development)
   - **People** (team and customer)
3 Prioritise the tasks according to their innovation impact.
4 Do this each week and always keep a balance between four areas.

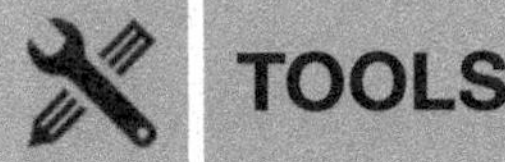

Task allocation

1 Create a grid, like the table on the next page.
2 Down the side put each action.
3 Along the top put who, what, when, where and how.
4 Think through and write down the best way to organise the activities that need to be accomplished, within each of the categories, in order to reach the vision.
5 How are you going to track your plan?

People actions	Who	When	Where	How
Action 1				
Action 2				

Results actions	Who	When	Where	How
Action 1				
Action 2				

Change actions	Who	When	Where	How
Action 1				
Action 2				

Process actions	Who	When	Where	How
Action 1				
Action 2				

SKILL TWO – Being able to see responsibilities through to completion

When we think of innovation, we often think of creativity – but, as we have already discussed, being creative, no matter how important, is only one part of being innovative. Being successful at taking an idea – retaining its novelty and creating value out of it – requires a complex raft of skills, capabilities and processes.

A few years back, we worked with a high growth technology business. They had a very innovative product and service offering and a committed leadership team that was focused on getting results. The challenge, however, was customer demand, a great challenge to have but only if you can keep pace and manage the stress on the operational aspect of delivering the service. Customer complaints were increasing and there were quality control issues. They could not cope. In analysing their data, the leadership team were high on skills associated with *identify* and *ignite* and, while they had employees that were high on *implement*, there was no one in the leadership team that was taking a methodical and painstaking approach to thinking through how they could make their service operational more effectively. Being systematic requires the ability to be methodical, detail-orientated, analytical and process-orientated and controlled. These qualities are vital in testing whether processes and procedures will generate consistent and optimal results and make innovation work.

ACTIVITY

Decide on priorities

1 Pick one of your goals.
2 Break it down into discrete activities.
3 Think of the interdependencies between all the activities. What needs to be done first?
4 Allocate how much time you think you will need for each task.
5 Prioritise what is urgent and what is important.
6 Pick an important activity and think through the best way to make it work.
7 Do that first. This will give you some energy and momentum when you start to see it move into action.
8 Be aware if you are just living in the urgent box all the time – this will wear you out.

ACTIVITY

Spend time with an implementer

1 Talk to someone who thinks more systematically than you do who is also action-orientated.
2 Ask them questions on how they approach activities. For example:
   - Tell me about how you approach your work. What do you do first?
   - Tell me in sequence what you do next.
   - What do you do when circumstances change? How do you factor in changes to your plans?
   - How do you get people to follow through on what they are responsible for?
3 What can you learn from them?
4 Incorporate one of their strategies into how you work.

SKILL THREE – Being able to see what could go wrong and know how to minimise risk

While innovating is often synonymous with risk taking, it does not mean that we blindly walk into the unknown. Part of *implementing* an idea is being good at managing risk. This requires being able to see ahead and think about where and when risks may appear and scenarios for the best way to minimise or reduce them. A lot of risks may have financial implications. If you are a small business invoicing for work from a large company with a 90-day payment policy, how are you going to cover the three months before you get paid? You may well have a great product or service, but cash is king and many a small venture has failed because they have not managed cash flow projection. Or, if you are working on a new venture in a large organisation that could potentially cannibalise current revenue streams from existing products and services, how are you going to manage the loss of potential income? Risk management requires a certain type of discipline. Being able to innovate, from a skills perspective, requires the curious combination of creativity and discipline, often seen as opposite ends of a spectrum. Creativity is a bit messy and unpredictable and discipline is about order and control, but you need both to do well. The art is knowing when to apply what skill and what mindset, with awareness.

TOOLS

Risk management

Brainstorm all the things that you think could go wrong with your plan:

- *Identify* the risks.
- *Analyse* them.
- *Rank* them in terms of impact.
- *Assess* options.
- Think through how you can *reduce* the risks.
- Proactively *manage* the risks.

Risk	Description	Rank (1 low risk, 10 high)	Options	Priorities	Actions

Create a board of advisors

1 Create a board of advisors; whether it is a lawyer, tax accountant, financial planner or someone in a profession that manages risks, ask them for their perspective.

2 If you are an entrepreneur, do you have the right insurance policies to protect yourself and your business? Ask for professional advice on what might be required.

SKILL FOUR – Being able to collaborate and build partnerships with others

'I don't seem to be able to get traction,' an aspiring entrepreneur said to me as we discussed how she could get her new business idea up and running. 'I get distracted by other ideas and can't seem to settle on one and see it through.' I was facilitating a Women Who Lead (WWL) retreat in Bali, which I hold a couple of times a year for female executives. A number of women, from all walks of life, were present. Some were CEOs, others small business owners; some were in between career choices and others directors in their respective domains. Each woman had arrived, stressed out from the demands of life and work, to spend uninterrupted time with an idea for a new project or business that they wanted to create. The aim of the retreat was to flesh out their ideas and work on the capabilities and skills that each would need to develop to allow them to step up to a new level of leadership and bring their ideas to life.

Looking through her Six 'I's® profile, the pattern became obvious. As a high *identifier* and *igniter*, this lady was not short on ideas; in fact, she was highly creative. Her *invest* and *implement* strengths were very low, however, causing her to bounce from idea to idea. This diluted her focus, and therefore her energy, not giving the time to move an idea into something concrete and practical.

It is one thing to have an idea and vision; it is another to make it happen. Yet, the skills of *implement* are often not seen as a valued part of the innovator's tool kit. They are critical. We created an *implementation* plan together and isolated key people in the networks of the retreat participants with whom she could, potentially, explore partnership opportunities.

TOOLS

Skills assessment

1 Go back to your plan.

- Under each activity, list the skills, capabilities and experience that you need to help your idea get traction.
- What skills do you have access to and what is missing?

Activity	Skills	Capabilities	Experience	Possible partners
Activity 1				
Activity 2				

2 What key people could help you make your idea work? These can be directly in your team and/or other important stakeholders. Why should they get involved to support you? (What is in it for them?)

3 Go through the key areas of your plan. Who may you need to partner to help you *implement* your idea?

- What type of support do you need? i.e. marketing, sales, product development, design, finance etc.
- Get advice on any areas that may involve legal agreements: formal joint ventures, alliances, etc.

DID YOU KNOW?

When Anita Roddick opened her first Body Shop® in 1976, she had no idea at just how successful it would become. She had *identified* a need for natural cosmetics that would appeal to her customers' concern for the environment. She *invested* a $6,500 loan and *ignited* ideas that addressed her need for low cost and also fit her environmental *Purpose*, offering discounted refills to customers, using minimal packaging to keep costs as low as possible. The business grew. To capitalise on expansion, and to raise *investment*, the Roddicks took The Body Shop® public in 1984. After just one day of trading, the stock doubled in value. By the end of 1992, she had *implemented* 700 Body Shop® stores, generating $231 million revenue.

But not all was easy and there were periods of declining sales and growing pains as she continued to *implement* her ideas. In 1996, the Roddicks brought in professional managers, installing tighter inventory control and streamlining processes. 'We've gone through a period of squashing one hell of a lot of the entrepreneurial spirit,' she told *Fortune* magazine. 'We're having to grow up; we have to get methods and processes in. And the result of that is a hierarchy that comes in and I think that's anti-productive.' This *implementation* failed to have the desired effect, and sales declined. After dismal financial performance in 1998, Roddick stepped down from being CEO and brought in Patrick Gourney to run the business. By 2004, The Body Shop® had 1,980 stores, serving over 77 million customers throughout the world. It was voted the second most trusted brand in the United Kingdom, and twenty-eighth top brand in the world. In March 2006, L'Oréal purchased The Body Shop® for $853 million and sold it in 2017 to a Brazilian cosmetics company, Natura Cosemitcos, owned by Aesop, for $1.6 billion, higher than analysts predicted. The innovation journey, for The Body Shop®, continues.

> 'If you think you're too small to have an impact, try going to bed with a mosquito.'
>
> *Anita Roddick*

What does this story illustrate? Anita Roddick had a very clear *Purpose* and she remained *committed* as she *implemented* her ideas. She had a strong vision and used the fact she did not have much money to *invest* to play to her *Purpose*. She remained *committed*, through the growing pains of professionalising the business. Through a combination of low-key marketing, consumer education and social activism, The Body Shop® rewrote the rulebook for the $16 billion global cosmetics business and made Roddick one of the richest women in England. The story continues, post her untimely death in 2007, and The Body Shop® brand has to continue to *identify* new opportunities and *ignite* ideas that they can *implement* into their market place.

SKILL FIVE – Being able to assemble teams with complementary skills and knowledge

We know that teaming is essential to successful innovation. As you become more aware of your own and others' strengths and learn how to work with different skills and experiences, you will increase your likelihood of success. When choosing people to partner, find out their Six 'I's® profile, and what you look like as a team. Too many *igniters*? You might have great fun generating new ideas, but who is going to focus on *implementation*?

There are many variables to take into consideration – temperament and personality preferences, experience and background, technical skill, the ability to communicate and build relationships, shared values – to name a few. Increasingly, work is dispersed geographically and virtual working is on the rise, so how will you manage that? The important thing is to go back to your *Purpose*. What are you trying to create and what is the problem you are trying to solve? Also, you may or may not be the right person to lead your innovation initiative now, but that may change. What type of leadership required at different stages of *implementation* will vary, but be ready to spot when change is required. The raft of skills, background, personalities and values will differ, depending on the nature of what it is you are trying to do. The important thing is to think about it consciously and plan for it.

The Six 'I's® Profile is not a personality tool, it is a skills strengths indicator that will give insight into yourself and other people's perceived innovation skills. Personality differences also impact our innovation style, so it is worth spending some time accelerating your awareness of your own and other's personalities as well, particularly if you are building teams. There are many different psychometric tools available to help you understand personality differences. A few that I have used with coaching clients and team building are Myers Briggs Type Indicator (MBTI), the Enneagram (Integrative9), and the Spony Profiling Model (SPM).

ACTIVITY

Team dynamics

1 Investigate different personality assessments that are available and choose one.

2 Work with an accredited practitioner, who is trained in the instrument, to get to know each other's similarities and differences and the impact this may have on how you work together.

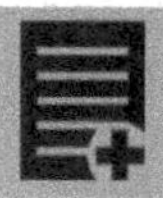

ACTIVITY

Team vision board

You may have created a vision board for yourself, but try creating one with the group of people you want to work with. This will help you collectively invent the future together.

1 In light of your collective vision, ask each person to create their own vision board of how they see themselves personally contributing.
2 How do each person's skills fit together as a whole?
3 What is missing?

TOOLS

Ways of working

Establish how you want to work with others:

1 Agree on the behaviours that you will hold each other to account on and think about when these might need to change depending on the stage of the innovation journey.
2 If you are working remotely, decide what online tools you will use and how and when you will have informal and formal online check-ins as well as face-to-face meetings.
3 Use the Grid to help create team alignment and a shared way of working.

SKILL SIX – Being able to help people complete their work in allocated budgets and timeframes

We may not like to speak of innovation and management in the same breath but, in fact, to be really successful at innovating, we need to be good at managing it, from idea, through to implementation and improvement. When I started working in this field many years ago, the tools and processes that I found for managing innovation were very technical in nature and developed mostly for research and development (R&D) and product development purposes. While these are appropriate in some instances, very few focused on people, process or service innovation.

What this book is focusing on is the human factor – the ability to mobilise skills and create the conditions that will motivate others – to create and implement something new. Managing innovation, whether you are managing yourself, a loose group of contributors or partners or trying to bring a new idea to life in an organisational context, requires the skill of knowing how to motivate people and keep them on track towards a common Purpose. Innovation, unlike some other forms of management, has the added complexity of the unknown. You are doing something new, so the stakes are higher for all concerned. Things get tough, things fail, and resources – time, money and skills, in particular – may be limited. One of the bigger concerns is the change in priorities – innovative ideas and projects that might have been a key area of focus fall off the radar in response to other pressures. The damage that this can do to individual and team motivation can be immense.

Six 'I's® Tracker

Use The Six 'I's® as an innovation management process.

1 At which 'I' is your idea?

2 Have you *identified* a clear opportunity?

3 Have you *ignited* an idea that can become a solution?

4 Have you *investigated* how it could work?

5 Have you got the necessary *investment*?

6 Are you ready to move into *implementation*?

If not, move back to the relevant 'I' and think about what needs to be done. Play to the strengths of your team's (or partner's) Six 'I's® profiles.

Use the following table to help you manage your ideas.

Stage of the Journey						
	Identify	Ignite	Investigate	Invest	Implement	Improve
Idea 1						
Idea 2						
Idea 3						
Idea 4						

ACTIVITY

Fit roles to motivations

Look at your and your team's personality results.

1 What motivates you and them?

2 How can you appeal to their motivations as well as their skills and abilities to keep them involved and energised?

Dangers of Missing Out the *IMPLEMENT* Stage

- You (or your team) may not have clear goals.
- There will be a lack of clarity on role and responsibilities.
- You will lack results orientation and a way to evaluate performance.
- Your ideas will stay as ideas and not move into value creation. Innovation will not be achieved.

THE IMPLEMENT MINDSET

'TO STAY COMMITTED DESPITE CHALLENGES AND BE DEDICATED TO ACHIEVING RESULTS'

COMMITTED

Imagine you are in a small boat with a group of people. The sun is shining and the water is calm. Laughter fills the air as you paddle down the river. Suddenly, the boat starts to rock and then spins around. You hit the rapids and the laughter stops. Soaked from the spray, and with a sense of exhilaration, you manage to steer the boat through the rapids, unaware that you have drifted off course and are heading straight to the edge of a waterfall. 'This one is going to be tough.' So I said to a group of people at TEDxSingapore in August 2010. My talk was called 'White Water

Leadership', likening our ability to innovate to the skills of white water rafting. While some rapids are easy to navigate, others are not.

Yet, we pick up the paddle and try again. There are days when we feel really low. There are days when we want to give up. But, who we are in the face of disappointment often can determine whether we succeed or fail. It can be lonely and, most likely, you will be misunderstood – until you are a success, that is, and then you will be praised. Being on the edge of something new – whether working inside an organisation, trying to influence your peers or working as an entrepreneur – most people will see you as a maverick, not quite fitting in with what they see as important or necessary.

Resilience and agility are the current buzz words of our time. But how do you teach such qualities? The only way is to have experiences. You cannot learn this from a textbook or a course. You have to go through the highs and lows of a life fully lived. You have to face disappointment, feel it in your bones and come out on the other side feeling stronger. You have to have faith in your vision and self-belief. You have to have confidence, oodles of it and, if one door shuts, you open another one. You do not give up.

Our ability to stay committed is largely determined by the amount of grit that we have. What is grit? It is the ability to pick oneself up in the face of great disappointment or failure and have another go. Or, as psychologist Angela Lee Duckworth says: 'Grit is sticking with your future – day in, day out, not just for the week, not just for the month, but for years – and working really hard to make that future a reality.'

Research is starting to show us that this notion of grit – passion and perseverance for long-term goals – is one of the highest determinants of both academic and professional success. The Duckworth Lab. at the University of Pennsylvania, has established the predictive power of grit. In longitudinal studies, it can predict who will survive arduous military training, be high academic achievers, and so on. Grit is far more powerful than IQ, levels of fitness, family income and even talent itself. Grit is ultimately about personality and character. It is that internal motor that just keeps on going.

So how can we get grittier? We may think that our characters and personalities hardly change. But research says, just like our brains, our personalities are not immutable and can adapt to new stimulus and experience.

Having intelligence or talent is just the starting point. What we need is a growth mindset. This mindset can only be developed through practice and applying one's thinking in a consistent way, despite the challenges or obstacles one may face. If we have a love of learning, and stay committed, we will build the muscle of resilience. This enables us to achieve results, to be accomplished. A growth mindset is a belief that the way that we think and the wiring of our neurones are not fixed. We can adapt to change, learn, and relearn and stay the course when things get tough. If we believe that failure, or to fail, is not a permanent condition we will discover that frustration and confusion are part of the learning process, rather than a sign that we should give up. We can stand up and try again, and again, and again.

Those most likely to persevere are those that believe failure is not a permanent condition. Instead, they accept frustration and confusion as part of the learning process, rather than a sign that they should give up. Both strategies increase the ability to have more commitment.

This brings us again to the importance of our early years. Like creativity, a growth and gritty mindset can be cultivated when children are young, when character is moulded. A British newspaper carried an interesting article on a school in Bedford, United Kingdom, that is actively pioneering the development of grit in its pupils. In addition to their academic achievements, students are graded on their character and behaviour.

There is a delicate balance, though, and one that is difficult to learn. Having a committed mindset does not always mean that you keep on going against the odds, doing what you have always done, even if it is not getting you the results you want. A committed mindset means that you will keep seeking new pathways to achieve your goals, even if the pathway you have to choose might take you in a different direction from what you originally intended. It is only with hindsight that we have the luxury to be able to look back on our decisions and make sense of them.

We also need to learn to recover, to get out of the boat and away from the rapids, and to pace ourselves. This is not about being a workaholic or slave driver. It is not about how many hours we push ourselves to achieve something. A burnt-out pioneer is no good to anyone, let alone oneself.

Even the most painful decisions or experiences we may make or have – losing a job, closing a company, making people redundant, letting go of a dream – can but serve to shape and mould the character and mindset of commitment.

Want to Develop a Committed Mindset?

To stay committed despite challenges and be dedicated to achieving results.

TRY THIS

1 Build Resilience

- When you feel like giving up on something, or want to quit, push through the feelings of despondency and make a decision to continue.
- Recount something where you feel you failed. Reframe the situation in your mind. How did you feel about it? Shame, guilt, frustration, fear, sadness, anger? What did you learn from the failure? What did it teach you?
- Next time you fail at something, tell yourself that it is not a permanent condition. It too will pass.
- When you are trying something new, and feel frustrated or confused, tell yourself it is all part of the learning process, not a signal to give up.
- Pick something that you are passionate about and that you want to learn. Dedicate time to it. Stay committed, even when you think you cannot do it. Push through your emotions that tell you it will not work. Studying 16,000 people, Angela Duckworth found that 'grittier people are *dramatically* more motivated than others to seek a meaningful, other-centred life'.

2 Time to Say No?

- Have you been committed to something for too long and you are not getting the results you want to see? Do not beat yourself up about it. Learn to let go and try something else. It is a fine line, but there is a difference between being committed and knowing when it is time to say 'enough'.
- If it is your passion, you *will* find another way.

3 Find a Mentor

- In his book, *Creativity: The Psychology of Discovery and Invention*, Mihaly Csikszentmihalyi interviewed over 91 of the most creative people in the world (including 14 Nobel Prize winners). What did they have in common? By the time they were college age, almost everyone had an important mentor.

- Find someone that will inspire you, give you guidance, act as an effective role model and offer you emotional support.

Make these *committed* mindset activities part of your life.

Ready to move on to *improve*? Revisit your Purpose Statement and use this simple checklist to make sure you have covered some of the most salient points of *implement*. Do you need to go back to *identify* or *invest*? How well is your proposition working?

Activity	Complete
I have a project plan in place with clear timelines and accountabilities. I have balanced activities across the four areas: *people*, *results*, *change* and *process*.	
I have prioritised actions that I need to take and am focused on the activities that will drive innovation impact.	
I have analysed and assessed the risks with what I want to do and am going forward with my eyes open to potential challenges. I have reduced the risks where I can.	
I have got a team in place and know what motivates them, as well as myself. We are in alignment on what we need to achieve and are committed to see results. I am practising developing grit and resilience.	

To dig deeper into developing the skill and mindset, refer to the resource guide at the end of this chapter, but first let us meet Christine Sim, whose highest score on The Six 'I's® is *implement*.

LET'S MEET CHRISTINE SIM

THE IMPLEMENTER PROFILE

Name:	Christine Sim
Job:	CEO
Company:	The Entre Club, Asia-Pacific
Primary Six 'I's® rating:	Implementer

What challenges are you looking to solve with innovation right now?

I am building a training and connectivity platform for young and growing businesses across Asia. It is a platform for synergistic collaboration. Our vision is to be a major economic force for sustainable growth and opportunity creation in Asia. We foresee a trend in working professionals moving out of corporate life to set up their own businesses, others are looking at how they can scale and grow the companies that they have already created, across the region. We aim to be a catalyst for positive change.

Looking at your Six 'I's® results, you're an *implementer*. How does this knowledge impact or change the way you work?

It helps me to see the big picture of any project as well as the micro components that need to be woven together to make it happen. I am able to break the vision down into sizeable chunks and prioritise them into what needs to be done so that we can build something that will be sustainable. It is like seeing the whole jigsaw puzzle in the mind first and then putting each individual piece together. I can visualise how each part can contribute to the whole.

How do you play to your strengths? What advice would you give other people who want to get better at *implementing*?

You need to have the end goal in mind. The only way you get good at implementing is to have a go at it, to get experience. A lot of people will not try, as they fear failure. I would encourage others to test out their idea and learn from the mistakes. It is about being a risk taker and seeking constant improvement. If you do not have your own idea to work on, where you can acquire first-hand learning, see if you can join a group that is launching a new initiative and get experience by working with them and learning from joint collaboration. Experience gives you expertise and expertise gives you confidence. Dare to try, as this will give you courage to do it for yourself. Be humble, take in feedback from others and learn from them by seeing what they do and how they do it. Collaborate, as this will allow you to focus your strengths, as any person's time and energy is finite. Focus and discipline are two keys for successful implementation.

What steps, if any, would you take to improve the areas where you are not so strong, or that are important to you and how?

I try to adapt my skills to the different situations that I am in. If I need to be stronger at *igniting* new ideas, then I consciously shift my mindset towards this. I continually ask for feedback from people that I have deep respect for and seek out mentors to guide me. I try to hold myself back from implementing too quickly by *investigating* ideas first to see if they will work – focus groups, discussions with customers, stakeholders, colleagues, mentors. I ask others who know how to do something that I cannot do, how they did it and how they can help me. This way I can continuously learn.

How has The Six 'I's® helped you and your teams/business? What examples, if any, can you share?

It has given me a new level of self-awareness about my innovation strengths. It is a practical tool and something that I can bring into my everyday work and daily life as well. The Six 'I's® has helped me to understand my strengths and my team members better. It has also helped me take a more integrative team approach to managing the successful delivery of projects in all areas of my life. I am currently an advisor to a group of young people who are launching a book about entrepreneurship in Singapore called https://whyyoushouldfail.com/, which is about how to build a profitable company that will last. Being more aware of The Six 'I's®, I could guide them to play to their strengths. This helped to create greater work synergy.

Have you produced something you would consider innovative?

In launching several mega projects in the past, I have learnt that, after planning, it is about hard work and determination. With regards to The Entre Club, to implement the vision of what we want to create requires great connections, particularly with senior mentors across the region who can coach and advise our potential members – it is truly about leaders multiplying leaders and creating success and legacy. The success pillars include resourcing, commercialisation, execution and delivery. Building the right team and resource network is critical to our expansion so that we can help others to unlock their potential and grow their entrepreneurial ventures. I have also approached my life with a mindset of reinvention – life is a state of constant innovation. I started my career as a secretary and I am now a CEO, but it is still a work in progress. I feel I am still evolving and reinventing myself to deal with life's changing circumstances. The ability to reinvent oneself, no matter where you are in life, is going to be increasingly critical in a world that is in constant flux, if one is to future-proof success and sustainability.

THE IMPLEMENT RESOURCE GUIDE

This section outlines some resources for further exploration to get better at implementing ideas and developing a committed mindset.

RESOURCE GUIDE

- Want to find out just how gritty you are? Take Professor Duckworth's questionnaire on the university's website: https://angeladuckworth.com/grit-scale/.
- Three psychological profiling tools I have found very insightful for team building are Myers Briggs Type Indicator (MBTI) www.mbtionline.com, the Spony Profiling Model (SPM) www.spmonline.eu (which measures the impact national culture has on leadership decision making) and the Enneagram www.integrative9.com, which creates self-awareness and uncovers patterns of behaviour across nine distinct personality types.
- There is a range of affordable project management software now available online. Here is a good blog that outlines 10 of the best: http://www.creativebloq.com/software/best-project-management-71515632
- Mindtools has lots of tips and tricks for developing new skills. Here is a good article on how to manage Stakeholders: www.mindtools.com/pages/article/newPPM_08.htm.

- Want to manage ideas? Here is a good overview of idea management software that is available online: www.capterra.com/idea-management-software/.
- Want an online platform that mirrors The Six 'I's® Model? We have partnered with Softools, a business app developer in the UK, to design a Six 'I's® Innovation Management platform. Highly flexible solutions with zero coding: www.softools.net.
- Want to find a great mentor? Here is a good book to help you: *Power Mentoring: How Successful Mentors and Protégés Get the Most Out of Their Relationships* by Ellen Ensher and Susan Murphy (2005).

FURTHER READING

There are plenty of books available on all the subjects listed below. Here are a few to help expand your thinking.

Getting to market

Anthony, S. (2014) *The First Mile: A Launch Manual for Getting Great Ideas into the Market*. Harvard Business Review Press.

Organising and planning

Allen, D. (2015) *Getting Things Done: The Art of Stress-free Productivity*. Piatkus.

Ferris, T. (2017) *The 4-Hour Work Week*. CreateSpace Independent Publishing Platform.

Lencioni, P. (2004) *Death by Meeting: A Leadership Fable about Solving the Most Painful Problem in Business*. John Wiley & Sons.

Service, O. and Gallagher, R. (2017) *Think Small: The Surprisingly Simple Ways to Reach Goals*. Michael O'Mara.

Tracy, B. (2013) *Eat that Frog: Get More of the Important Things Done Today*. Hodder Paperbacks.

Zogby, J.P. (2017) *The Power of Time Perception: Control the Speed of Time to Make Every Second Count*. Time Lighthouse Publishing.

Project management

Newton, R. (2007) *Project Management Step by Step: How to Plan and Manage a Highly Successful Project*. Pearson Business.

Sutherland, J. (2015) *Scrum: The Art of Doing Twice the Work in Half the Time.* Random House Business.

Innovation management

Tidd, J. and Bessant, J. (2013) *Managing Innovation: Integrating Technological, Marketing and Organizational Change*. John Wiley & Sons.

von Stamm, B. (2008) *Managing Innovation, Design and Creativity*. Wiley.

Marketing and sales

Cakim, I.M. (2010) *Implementing Word of Mouth Marketing: Online Strategies to Identify Influencers, Craft Stories, and Draw Customers.* John Wiley & Sons.

Heath, C. and Heath, D. (2007) *Made to Stick: Why Some Ideas Survive and Others Die*. Random House.

Priestly, D. (2015) *Oversubscribed: How to Get People Lining Up to Do Business with You*. Captsone.

Building teams

Kostner, J. (1996) *Virtual Leadership: Secrets From the Round Table for the Multi-site Manager*. Time Warner International.

Lencioni, P. *The Five Dysfunctions of a Team: A Leadership Fable.*

Performance

Duckworth, A. (2017) *Summary of Grit: The Power of Passion and Perseverance.* CreateSpace Independent Publishing Platform.

Ericsson, A. (2016) *Peak: Secrets from the New Science of Expertise.* Eamon Dolan/Houghton Mifflin Harcourt.

Pink, D. (2011) *Drive: The Surprising Truth about What Motivates Us.* Canongate Books Ltd.

IMPROVE

OPTIMISE, SCALE AND LEARN FROM SUCCESS AND FAILURE

'Could you look at creating a talent development project in China where local HR managers could facilitate the Model on innovation projects?' I was asked by a client. We had been eight years in Asia and The Six 'I's® had begun to extend into the original *Purpose* that I had when I created it. 'How about an online tool kit where individuals, dispersed in global teams across the world, could access innovation tools to apply to new business challenges?' said another.

Many ideas for *improvement* have come with the practical use and application of the Model on real organisational challenges, others at the request from clients. When I reflect back over my innovation journey in creating The Six 'I's®, what started off as a simple circular diagram has now become a suite of online applications, profiling instruments, certification programmes, merchandising, tool kits and games. It has been, and continues to be, a journey of continuous *improvement*, going backwards and forwards across the six stages of the Model. In collaborating with clients, we have been able to *investigate* through prototyping and developing new applications that directly meet their needs and, in so doing, meet the needs of other organisations. And we continue to keep *investing*, *implementing* and *improving* what we have by extending the original idea into other *identified* areas of opportunity. We now have a product development pipeline that will take us far into the future.

It was as if what could have been seen as a set of random events and experiences of my life came together – strategising new markets for learning, being employed in a large research organisation, digital product development, my love of psychology and culture, training, facilitating and consulting, plus the network of contacts that I had developed over time – combined to give a launch pad to build something that has been of value to many individuals and organisations around the world.

We all sit on a mountain of value – our experience, knowledge, skills and networks – yet often we do not see what is right before our eyes. We do not see what we can *improve* and how we can maximise and leverage what we already have. Many individuals and organisations can bypass this very rich and rewarding phase of innovation altogether, chasing after another idea and missing the low-hanging fruit of opportunity that stares them in the face. Sometimes, in our initial vision, we can see what the possibilities are, but we lose sight of them amidst the difficulties and challenges of trying to make a new idea work. While chronologically, *improve* is the last 'I' we have discussed, The Six 'I's® is not a linear process. It is a circular Model, and *improve* can often be the starting point for doing something new.

I share this story to illustrate how what started out as a simple idea for just a conceptual model has grown into something far more valuable, and is now even the subject of this book that you are reading. *Improve*, how to maximise and leverage ideas, is the subject for this chapter.

Throughout, I will give examples of practical ways to help boost your ability and confidence to *improve* on ideas.

Improve is central to innovation, for it can often bring quick ways of generating more value out of something that already exists. The *improve* phase of innovation involves being able to generate many ways to make an idea better and seeking opportunities to *improve* on ideas with a variety of people, customers or stakeholders. This is important as innovative outcomes can often be generated from optimising and extracting more value out of an idea that already exists. It is the end user, or customer, who can often give the best suggestions on how something could be improved.

Capturing learning so that there is continuous improvement and creating a culture where people can learn from failure are also important as they encourage individuals and groups to reflect on their own behaviour and learn from the past.

Like *investigate*, the freedom to experiment and, therefore, potentially fail, is part of the *improve* phase. It requires discovering new ways of doing things through trial and error. It is about building a mindset of learning into the whole of the innovation journey and the way that we work.

Reviewing and assessing what has worked and why or why not, and communicating successes and lessons learned, can help to create a culture of continuous improvement. Bringing learning to life, through the power of story, will also enable you to weave together your experiences in a memorable way. To be good at *improve* requires a *clever* mindset.

THE IMPROVER PROFILE

Innovation role – Providing fresh perspectives, the ability to optimise and learn
Mindset – Clever

Improver's strengths:

1. Being good at generating many ways to make an idea better.
2. Being open to gathering feedback from customers, people, or stakeholders.
3. Reviewing and assessing what has worked and why or why not?
4. Capturing learning.
5. Learning from failure.
6. Scaling an idea into other areas of opportunity.

The image represents the mindset of being ***Clever****. The swirl starts to open up on itself again to start seeking and exploring how it can do something better.*

Improver's challenges

As improvers largely work with what is, rather than what could exist, they may:

- Find it difficult to imagine completely new possibilities.
- Rely on continuous improvement.
- Miss opportunities for more radical ideas.
- Be fearful of moving too far away from the knowledge of what they think will work.

The challenge for *improvers* is that many organisations and individuals often like to jump into the next activity, rather than reflect on what they have already learned. *Improvers* need to help people actively learn from how they are innovating, both from success and failure.

HOW TO COMMUNICATE WITH *IMPROVERS*

Depending on the combination of 'I's on someone's profile, here are a few do's and don'ts that will help you communicate more effectively with *improvers*.

Do's	Don'ts
Talk about improvement, learning and optimisation of existing ideas.	Forget to review and assess or see new possibilities for what already exists.
Include them in brainstorming sessions, particularly if you are trying to improve existing products, services or processes.	Undermine the importance of their contribution to learning from mistakes and failures, as well as what has worked. Act on this knowledge.
Involve them in soliciting feedback from customers, end users or stakeholders.	Put them in roles that lack scope for further improvement or development.
Solicit their opinion on what would work better and why.	Move on to another project or activity without extracting ideas for further optimisation.

THE IMPROVE SKILLS

While there are many skills that help us to *improve* ideas, we will focus on six core attributes critical to this phase of innovation:

1 To analyse what has contributed to making something work or fail
2 To gather feedback from customers
3 To scale an idea into other areas of opportunity
4 To help others learn from things that didn't work out
5 To create a culture of continuous learning
6 To share positive outcomes and lessons learnt

Let us look at each one in turn.

Below is a top-line summary of the skills and their associated tools and activities for the area of *improve*.

Skills	Tools	Activities
To analyse what has contributed to making something work or fail	After Action Review (AAR)	Team reflection
To gather feedback from customers		Involve customers
To scale an idea into other areas of opportunity	SCAMPER	Extend your ideas
To help others learn from things that didn't work out	Attitudes to failure	
To create a culture of continuous learning		Capture learnings
To share positive outcomes and lessons learnt	Recognition and communication review	

SKILL ONE – Being able to analyse what has contributed to making something work or fail

Think of yourself looking into a mirror for a few seconds and seeing your face reflecting back, or gazing into a pool of water and seeing the scenery behind you shimmering on the surface edge. You are able to see things that maybe you had not noticed before. You gain a different perspective. Yet, many working cultures only reward activity and action. We are taught from a young age to be busy and productive, to move on to the next set of actions that need to be accomplished. We are not taught or encouraged to review our actions and, less so, our behaviour. Yet, in this reflection and review lies a wealth of wisdom and learning. To reflect is an activity in itself, even if it requires us to stop. This has to be actively pursued. It also requires a degree of maturity and honesty. If you are going to review, with the intention of learning, you have to be brutally honest with yourself and with others as to why something has worked or not. There also has to be responsibility and accountability rather than an excuse or blame culture. When we are trying to bring new ideas into the world, a lot of what we try may fail, or may not go as we originally planned, other times things may go a lot better than we could have anticipated or expected. We need to be able to learn from it all, whether we consider it a success or not.

ACTIVITY

Team reflection

Within a project, and when you come to the end of a project, reflect back on what you have learnt regarding *how* you worked – particularly if you were working with other people.

- What worked well?
- What did not work well?

This will help you be more aware of the circumstances that helped you innovate so that you can try and replicate or bypass these in the future.

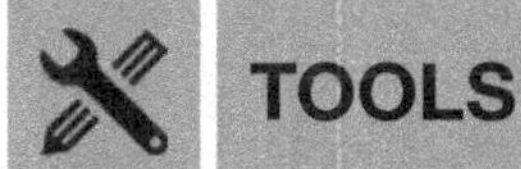

After Action Review (AAR)

1 Conduct an after action review (AAR) – originally developed by the US Army – and use these questions to help guide you:
   - What was supposed to happen?
   - What actually happened?
   - Why was there a difference?
   - What can we learn from this?
2 Identify, discuss and put in place actions to sustain the successes and to learn from and improve upon the failures. If you are having an AAR as a group, see if someone else can facilitate your discussion, so that you can all contribute.
3 Capture and write up your learnings.

SKILL TWO – Being able to analyse what has contributed to making something work or fail

Many of the tools and tips outlined in this book can be used at different phases of the innovation journey. This particular skill – being able to seek opportunities to improve on an idea with a variety of people, customers and stakeholders – can deploy approaches that we outlined in the *investigate* phase. The people that are engaging with your products and services are often the ones that can help you to *improve* what you are doing. They know if things work or not, as they are closer to the user experience. Gathering feedback is one thing, but companies that are doing this really well are deploying a range of activities to involve their customers in the *improve* phase of innovation and, in so doing, are starting to *identify* completely new opportunities for *igniting* new ideas. It is not just companies that create consumer products either, but business-to-business providers such as DHL, the world's largest mail and logistics services company and DeWalt, a leading manufacturer of high-quality power tools, that actively engage their customers in product and service innovation. Over 6,000 customer engagements have been conducted with loyal DHL customers, resulting, according to Forbes, in customer satisfaction scores rising to over 80 per cent, on-time delivery performance increasing to 97 per cent and a decrease in customer churn. DeWalt has an award-winning insight community of more than 10,000 users where they gather customer product, packaging and marketing feedback. They also invite professional tradesmen and loyal customers to submit ideas for entirely new product lines.

ACTIVITY

Involve customers

1 Look back over your project:
   - What potential customers or stakeholders did you engage to help you test your propositions?
   - Have they become customers or users of what you have created?
   - What has this process been like for them?

2 How could you engage these people in the *improvement* process?
   - Ask them for feedback.
   - What do they like, not like about what you have created?
   - What ideas do they have for further *improvement*?

3 If you are developing online products or services, you have a wealth of user data that you can use to see actively how people are engaging, real time, with what you have on offer. Analyse these data and see what *improvements* you can make.

SKILL THREE – Being able to scale an idea into other areas of opportunity

Back in 2004, a book was written called *The Wisdom of the Crowds: Why the Many Are Smarter Than the Few and How Collective Wisdom Shapes Business, Economies, Societies and Nations* by James Surowiecki. The main premise of the book is that the collective judgement of a group of people may be preferable to the view of a much smaller, albeit brighter, less diverse group of experts. This idea of collective intelligence – amidst the rise of user-generated media such as blogs, Wikipedia and YouTube – has spurred a plethora of business models that enable organisations to collaborate online. The traditional distinction between producers and consumers is being eroded, which is giving rise to new ways of engaging people in the innovation process.

One such practice is crowdsourcing – the ability to tap into the creative intelligence of customers or potential customers through online platforms. Crowdsourcing has additional benefits in addition to soliciting feedback for *improvement*; it can also *improve* productivity by minimising labour and research expenses, reducing the amount of time spent collecting data through formal focus groups or trend research. Crowdsourcing is also an excellent approach for gathering input into the development of new ideas for the *ignite* phase. For example, Netflix, the online video rental service, deploys crowdsourcing techniques to improve the software algorithms used to offer customer video recommendations. The team or individual that achieves key software goals receives $1 million. Procter & Gamble taps 90,000 chemists on Innocentive.com, a forum where scientists collaborate with companies to solve R&D problems in return for cash prizes.

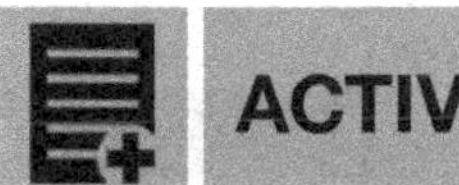

ACTIVITY

Extend your idea

1 Look at what you have created.
   - How could you optimise the idea further?
   - How could you *improve* it?
   - List 10 different ways in which you could use your idea in different markets or customer groups.

2 How could you tap into the wisdom of a crowd?
   - Investigate different crowdsourcing platforms and see what might be relevant for you.

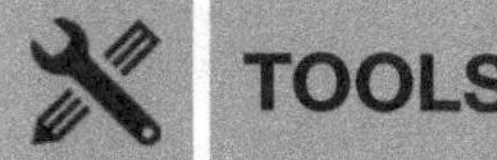

TOOLS

Scamper

A simple, but practical, tool that is useful to help think about how to *improve* products, services or processes is a methodology called SCAMPER, developed by Bob Eberle, an education administrator and author.

Look at your innovation:

- What could you **S**ubstitute?
- What could you **C**ombine?
- What could you **A**djust?
- What could you **M**odify?
- What could you **P**ut to another use?
- What could you **E**liminate?
- What could you **R**everse or **R**earrange?

Use SCAMPER to help think of different ways to *improve* on your idea or proposition.

DID YOU KNOW?

In 2003, LEGO – based in a Danish village called Billund and owned by the same family that founded it before World War Two – was on the verge of bankruptcy. Faced with growing competition from video games and the internet, and plagued by a fear that it was perceived as out of touch with its customers, the company had made a series of management errors and detours away from its core areas of competence. Even its most successful products – including Star Wars and Harry Potter lines – were dependent on movie release schedules and therefore out of LEGO's control. Stockpiles of LEGO toys lay unsold within stores around the world. In 2004, 36-year-old Jorgen Big Knudstorp was promoted as CEO and began to turn the company around. His *improvement* was on two levels – internal – improving processes, cutting costs that did not add value to the customer and managing cash flow – and external, getting to know the heart and soul of how kids play, which he did through commissioning deep ethnographic studies and deploying design thinking approaches. LEGO also used crowdsourcing to help *improve* and *ignite* new ideas. Within an online community, LEGO fans all over the world can discover other people's creations and offer feedback for improvement. They can also vote on submissions. If a project gets 10,000 votes, LEGO reviews the idea, picks a winner and develops and distributes it globally. The creator of the idea earns a percentage of sales and is recognised on LEGO packaging and marketing.

www.fastcompany.com/3040223/when-it-clicks-it-clicks and www.visioncritical.com/5-examples-how-brands-are-using-co-creation/

SKILL FOUR – Being able to help others learn from things that didn't work out

You may well hire or work with people that have a propensity to experiment and learn but, if the culture of your organisation or team does not support experimentation, even in a measured way, it really does not matter what attitude or mindset individual employees may well have. If culture is made up of the underlying attitudes and values intrinsic to how things get done, then creating a culture where people can learn from failure means we need to understand these underlying aspects that shape how an organisation thinks. No easy task. I often get asked how organisations can build a more innovative culture. It is a valid but difficult question to answer, as culture is something that is multi-faceted, involves history and legacy, and includes a set of deeply held beliefs. It is one thing to have a list of values that may incorporate the word innovation, on the wall or published in a corporate annual report. It is yet another to live and breathe innovation in daily activities – what I would call 'day-to-day innovation', challenging assumptions and doing things differently. So how can it be done? At the top, leaders have to ensure that innovation, the creation and implementation of new ideas, is intertwined and integrated into the very fabric of the company's strategic direction and that the permission to fail is built into, even expected, when it comes to trying out new things. It is also reframing what we mean by failure, within the context of innovation. If people know that there is a process to innovation, a journey that an idea goes through, they will be more likely to know and understand that trying out new ideas involves experimentation.

TOOLS

Attitudes to failure

1 Be honest about your own attitude towards failure. Paul Schoemaker, former research director, at Wharton's Mack Institute, outlines five attitudes. Pick the number that best fits you. If you do not know, ask someone else what they think you are.

Number	Attitude
1	I hate mistakes, hide them quickly, learn little from them, and will likely repeat the same error again in the future.
2	If I can't hide the mistake, I do try to analyse what happened and whom to blame; so some learning occurs, but it is mostly finger pointing and ego protection.
3	I generally welcome well-intentioned mistakes in myself and others; I strongly feel we should give recognition awards at work to people who failed for the right reasons.
4	I rank long-term learning higher than short-term results and fully accept that embracing mistakes is part of the package; I try to celebrate insights gleaned from errors.
5	I have actually made mistakes on purpose at times, by trying things that went against my best judgment, just to see if my thinking was perhaps flawed in this case.

Source: https://www.inc.com/paul-schoemaker/brilliant-failures/why-failure-is-the-foundation-of-innovation.html

The higher the number you have picked, the more open you are to experiment. From a survey Schoemaker conducted at Wharton Executive Education, most people (74 per cent) circled answers near or below the middle of the scale, namely 2 or 3. Clearly, many managers still have some way to go in developing a more open attitude to failure, as further explained in Schoemaker's book *Brilliant Mistakes: Finding Success on the Far Side of Failure*.

2 To gauge your team or organisation's attitude to failure, replace the 'I' for 'We'. Which number would you pick? What does that reveal about your culture and how it impacts your ability to innovate?

SKILL FIVE – Being able to create a culture of continuous learning

Societies and economies are less and less dependent on the manufacturing of physical goods as intangible products and services take more and more of the share of global trade. This makes the creation and application of knowledge increasingly important, whether it can be codified or stored (explicit) or whether it is difficult to transfer to others by writing it down (tacit). The average amount of time someone stays within a job is reducing, particularly amongst younger people, and, when they walk out of the door – their knowledge, networks and other forms of social capital – walk out with them. We also do not know what we do not know. If you work in a large organisation, you do not know what is happening in another part of the company. With the rate and pace of change as it is, certain types of knowledge can become redundant quickly, outdated or of little use. This makes the active capture and sharing of learning all the more necessary, in the moment, particularly when you are trying to do something new.

The goal is to create a culture where an attitude of continuous improvement is the norm, throughout the whole of the innovation journey, not just at the end. What we need to nurture and develop, in ourselves and others, is the skill of learning and unlearning – of having an agile mind that is willing to shift direction when new understanding and knowledge becomes available.

Capture learnings

1 How can you formally capture explicit learning?
   - If you are in a large organisation, are there online platforms that you could utilise to specifically manage and share knowledge related to innovation?
   - If you are a small business or entrepreneur, explore the range of online applications that can help teams share knowledge, for free, or at a low cost.

2 To ensure that you are capturing learning that is harder to write down or store – tacit or implicit knowledge that emerges through group and team activity – build in personal and team activities where people can share and build on each other's observations and insights.

3 Check out online platforms that can enable collaborative working and knowledge sharing. Do some research; find a service that fits your *Purpose*.

SKILL SIX – Being able to share positive outcomes and lessons learnt

I often ask clients if they spend time celebrating or acknowledging successes and lessons they have learned. Many do not. Task-orientated and busy, they have moved on to the next project or initiative without looking back at what has been accomplished, whether good or bad. Yet, here lies a great opportunity for improvement, not just improvement of what has been done, but an opportunity for people to think consciously about what they have achieved and to celebrate it together. This is about culture building. It is about actively making the time to communicate with people and keep them involved and engaged. Acknowledging their contribution and the importance of their skills to making something work. This can help people see the journey that they have been on – what often started as an opportunity or a vague idea – into the creation of something that has tangible worth. Recognition. Valuing others. Praise. Gratefulness. Being thankful. Not really words we associate much with working life but, if we want to create a motivational climate where people are willing to invest their skills and talents, this type of recognition and communication can help to create the climate that can produce successful innovation outcomes.

TOOLS

Recognition and communication review

1 **Recognise**

- What makes you/your team members feel recognised? (Praise, reward, etc.)
- What could you do to improve your ability to communicate and engage with others to improve this sense of recognition?
- Start to formally recognise people for their contribution to helping new ideas become reality.

2 **Communicate**

- Start making communication and engagement part of the way that you formally and informally manage.
- Thank people for their contribution.
- Experiment with formal recognition incentives such as award ceremonies and innovation days – find out what works for you and the culture in which you work.
- Reinforce a commitment to innovation in organisational or team communications:
  a Company announcements
  b Newsletters
  c External communication with customers or clients

3 **Measure**

- Measure your innovation effectiveness that is appropriate for your industry and size of organisation.
- Actively communicate how you are going to track performance against innovation goals.

Name	Recognition requirements	How to motivate and communicate	Actions	Measures
Person 1				
Person 2				

Dangers of Missing Out the *IMPROVE* Stage

- You (or your team) might miss out on opportunities that could create faster value.
- You won't consciously recognise key learnings that could help you develop.
- You may ignore the importance of celebration and its impact on motivation.
- The compounded positive impact of many day to day innovations will be unnoticed and unacknowledged.

THE IMPROVE MINDSET

'TO BE MENTALLY BRIGHT, HAVING SHARP OR QUICK INTELLIGENCE'

CLEVER

It is no mistake that the last mindset of The Six 'I's® is *clever*. Being *clever* is required throughout the whole of the innovation journey, but there is something about this phase of innovating, when you are trying to maximise what you already have, that needs this particular type of orientation – a keen, sharp mind that is awake and mentally bright. Think of how Apple leverages its existing product range – different colours, different sizes, different memory capacities, incremental as well as radical improvements – creating more and more value out of the same idea. Or IKEA with its focus on cost reduction through improvements in robotic manufacturing and flat packing – making arm rests detachable, tweaking handle design on mugs, doubling the number of products that can be fitted on a pallet, thus reducing transportation costs. Examples abound and, while we may not see these smaller improvements as innovation, their cumulative effect can be astounding in terms of value creation. The profitability of the iPhone, securing 103.6 per cent of the smart phone industry's profits in the third quarter of 2016, and the sheer number of BILLY bookcases sold by IKEA, over 60 million in the world – nearly one for every hundred people – are examples of the importance of this *clever* mindset and a focus on improvement. But no organisation, not even Apple or IKEA, can rest on their laurels or think that the past secures the future. History teaches us otherwise. This makes the mindset of being *clever* all the more important.

Just imagine, if we all had this mindset when we turned up at work or started new projects, of constantly looking for how we could do things differently or do things better, what a collective impact we would have. Of being sharp, switched on, awake and alert – how much more personal satisfaction would we gain? How much more would we contribute to the organisations and teams with whom we work?

This is why I want to debunk the myth that I see in many organisations, that being innovative is only about being radical or creative or if you happen to work in research and development or new technology, or if you work in an innovation lab or department, or a brand new startup. Being innovative is so much more, and open to all, everyone can and must contribute. In fact, innovation needs to come from everywhere.

Sometimes, we think it is easy if you work in a small and nimble business to be *clever* and responsive and fast to adapt but, what if you work for a large organisation with all its legacy systems, bureaucracy and history? One of the best and most ambitious examples I have come across, that is well documented, of a large organisation with a *clever* mindset, is the story of white goods manufacturer Whirlpool. Back in the 1990s, faced with increasing competition and pressure from shareholders, Whirlpool's leaders created the vision of a business that would encourage 'innovation from everyone, everywhere'. This meant innovation across the board – products, customer touch points, business methods with suppliers and vendors, processes as well as its overall strategic focus. New ways of working included enrolling every salaried employee in an online course on business innovation, training 600 innovation mentors, setting aside a substantial share of capital spending every year for projects that were truly innovative and requiring every product-development plan to contain a sizeable component of new-to-market innovation. Also, one sure way to put innovation at the top of the agenda was to make it a large component of top management's long-term bonus plan. Even today, it continues to lead the way in its industry, particularly in environmental innovation being the first manufacturer to produce Energy Star products that save electricity and offer customers more value for money.

Of course, it takes commitment. Having this commitment to being *clever* is ongoing and needs nurturing and development by managers, leaders and all employees. While important to build awareness and skill, it is not just about sending people on training courses to become more innovative, it is about getting down into the processes, the systems, the values and beliefs about how things operate and having a commitment to making innovation central to all ways of working. It is not about having a campaign on innovation for a few months and then moving on to the next management fad. If we are to be *clever* – bright, with a sharp and quick intelligence – we need to think about how we can harness our skills and strengths to create more value for ourselves and the people and organisations with whom we work.

So, you have traversed the journey of The Six 'I's of Innovation®. Whether you have read this book through from cover to cover or have just read particular areas of interest, I hope that it has given you a digest of different perspectives, with tips and tools that you can practically apply in your own life. More importantly, I hope that it has broadened your world view of what it means to be innovative and shown you how to contribute your skills and talents, inspiring you to say, 'Yes, I can Innovate!'

Want to develop a clever mindset?

To be mentally bright, having sharp or quick intelligence.

TRY THIS

1 **Daily reflection** Build this practice into your day-to-day life. One simple way to do this is to ask yourself three questions at the end of each day:
   - What did I learn from today?
   - What did I contribute towards today?
   - If I had today again, what would I do differently and why?

These three simple, but powerful, questions will help you to build a mindset of continuous learning and improvement.

2 **Keep a work journal** Here are some insightful questions for building self-awareness. They are also good to encourage mental downtime, so you can give some space for your brain to process what it is learning:

- What events stand out in my mind from the workday and how did they affect my inner work life?
- What progress did I make today and how did it affect my inner work life?
- What catalysts or nourishing things did I do that supported me today? How can I sustain them tomorrow?
- What one thing can I do to make progress on my important work tomorrow?
- What setbacks did I have today and how did they affect my inner work life? What can I learn from them?
- What toxins and inhibitors affected me and my work today? How can I weaken or avoid them tomorrow? www.inc.com/jessica-stillman/why-you-should-keep-a-work-journal.html

3 **Mental stimulation**

- Play Scrabble or chess.
- Buy a book of crosswords and do one a day.
- Learn a new language.
- Read one book of fiction a month.

4 **Hang out with smart people**

- Think of the five people that you spend the most time with. Are they smarter than you?
- Find some more people you can add to your friendship group who challenge your thinking.

Make these *clever* mindset activities part of your life.

Use this simple checklist to make sure you have covered some of the most salient points of *improve*.

Activity	Complete
I have reviewed what I have done, what worked well and what did not and have captured my learnings for future projects.	
I have involved customers and stakeholders in reviewing what I have created and received feedback, insights and new ideas.	
I have optimised my ideas by finding ways that I can improve and leverage what I have created with other customers or in other places.	
I have built the practice of personal reflection into my life and am actively improving my *clever* mindset by seeing how I can *improve* on ideas.	

To dig deeper into developing the skill and mindset, refer to the resource guide at the end of this chapter, but first let us meet Rose Shapley, whose highest score on The Six 'I's® is *improve*.

LET'S MEET ROSE SHAPLEY

IMPROVER PROFILE

Name:	Rose Shapley
Job:	Product and service analyst
Company:	IRT – Illawarra Retirement Trust, Australia
Six 'I's® primary rating:	Improver

What challenge are you looking to solve with innovation right now?

We're a community-owned organisation that improves the lives of older people. We do this through our communities and services, and IRT Foundation. The retirement living and aged care market place is changing rapidly. For us to survive and grow we need not just new products and services, but completely new ways of meeting customer needs so people can live well for as long as they can.

Looking at your Six 'I's® results, you're an *improver*. How does this knowledge impact or change the way you work?

It has helped me to direct my strengths. My team members are high on the first three 'I's, so I feel I balance them out and help them see from a different perspective, as do they for me. I work well with what already exists rather than coming up with new ideas. I don't feel frustrated any more about not having original ideas. I don't have to be good at everything.

How do you play to your strengths? What advice would you give other people who want to get better at *improve*?

It is important to consider all the elements of the problem you are trying to solve and realise that one small change will have an impact. It is also really important to involve customers, as well as internal staff, in the process of improvement so you get their input. Improving on what exists can create more value quickly. It is also about thinking of the different ways that you can *improve* on an idea – from product or service extension, to leveraging new sources of revenue, improving processes or efficiencies – there are so many different ways one can *improve* an idea.

What steps, if any, would you take to improve the areas where you are not so strong or that are important to you and how?

I am trying to improve my ability to *identify*, as we need this skill so we can see what opportunities might emerge for us. I am doing this by working with people who are good at making sense of trends and patterns and understanding how they reach their conclusions. I find myself applying my *improve* skills in a different way and am starting to see how I can *identify* new opportunities for *improvement*. This helps to open up my thinking.

How has The Six 'I's® helped you and your teams/business? What examples, if any, can you share?

It has given us a common language and a consistent approach to innovation initiatives. It has also helped day-to-day innovation too, it's not just for innovation projects, but applying The Six 'I's® as a way of thinking about how to approach doing new things at work. For example, I created a check list for people in the organisation to help them think about how they are innovating using The Six 'I's® framework, which has helped them in their day-to-day projects. It doesn't have to be just for big initiatives.

Have you produced something you would consider innovative?

We are *identifying* many new opportunities for innovation, some which are quite radical and will work to change the business model of how people are cared for in their older years. But, one incremental, smaller initiative that I have been involved in, that emerged from an idea in one of our care centres, is about providing tablets (iPad, etc.) for residents to reduce isolation and open up communication channels for them. The problem was that the residents didn't know how to use the iPads. I set up a project to *identify* their needs and *investigate* what products and services were already available and then worked to *improve* on how the different ideas could work by testing out how residents interacted with the technology. Part of this was teaching them how to use the tablets and seeing what they found interesting and useful. Their main frustrations were around how to access information and keep in touch with their families. We're considering how the innovation can be *implemented* to create value for us as an organisation, as well as value for our residents in enriching their lives through increasing connectivity. Something important to consider in this example is that the way we used The Six 'I's® framework was not necessarily in a sequential format, as we shifted from *investigate* to *improve* a number of times to develop the idea.

THE IMPROVE RESOURCE GUIDE

This section outlines some resources for further exploration to help you *improve* ideas and develop a *clever* mindset committed to constant learning.

RESOURCE GUIDE

- Jeff Howe, a contributing editor to *Wired* magazine, first coined the term 'crowdsourcing' in a June 2006 article. Check out his blog: crowdsourcing.com.
- Don Tapscott, a well-known business thinker, is a proponent for mass collaboration in his book, *Wikinomics: How Mass Collaboration Changes Everything* (2007, Atlantic Books).
- A useful guide to crowdsourcing sites for small businesses: www.designhill.com/design-blog/top-10-best-crowdsourcing-sites-of-2016-for-your-business/.
- Hear from Professor Rita McGrath, faculty at Columbia Business School Executive Education, on why companies should think about the notion of failure differently: www.youtube.com/watch?v=gUKyxa4EPG0&feature=youtu.be.
- A good article which outlines some thought-provoking questions for how to effectively use SCAMPER: www.mindtools.com/pages/article/newCT_02.htm.
- Want to develop a more reflective way of seeing them sign up for one of the Writing Our Way Home e-courses: www.writingourwayhome.com/e-courses/.

- Keep an 'I done' list. Spending a few moments reflecting on what you achieved increases your energy as it releases happy endorphins in your brain. Making progress – even small wins – on meaningful work is a powerful motivator.
- Check out 'The Busy Person's Guide to the Done List': http://try.idonethis.com/the-busy-persons-guide-done-list/.

FURTHER READING

There are plenty of books available on all the subjects listed here. Here are a few to help expand your thinking.

Risk and failure

Schulz, K. (2011) *Being Wrong: Adventures in the Margin of Error*. Ecco.

Sundheim, D. (2013) *Taking Smart Risks: How Sharp Leaders Win When Stakes Are High*. McGraw-Hill Education.

Weinzimmer, L.G. and McConoughey (2012) *The Wisdom of Failure: How to Learn the Tough Leadership Lessons Without Paying the Price.* Jossey-Bass.

Company case studies

Snyder, N. and Duarte, D.L. (2008) *Unleashing Innovation: How Whirlpool Transformed an Industry*. Jossey-Bass.

Womack, J., Jones, D. and Roos, D. (2007) *The Story of Lean Production: Toyota's Secret Weapon in the Global Car Wars That Is Now Revolutionizing World Industry.* Free Press.

Agile and lean thinking

Imai, M. (2012) *Gemba Kaizen: A Commonsense Approach to a Continuous Improvement Strategy*. McGraw-Hill Education.

Meyer, P. (2015) *The Agility Shift: Creating Agile and Effective Leaders, Teams and Organisations*. Routledge.

Womack, J. and Jones, D. (2003) *Lean Thinking: Banish Waste and Create Wealth in Your Corporation*. Productivity Press.

Learning and reflection

Amabile, T. (2011) *The Progress Principle: Using Small Wins to Ignite Joy, Engagement, and Creativity at Work*. Harvard Business Review Press.

Duhigg, C. (2014) *The Power of Habit: Why We Do What We Do in Life and Business*. Random House Trade Paperbacks.

Kegan, R. and Laskow Lahey, L. (2016) *An Everyone Culture: Becoming a Deliberately Developmental Organisation*. Harvard Business Review Press.

Senge, P. (2006) *The Fifth Discipline: The Art & Practice of the Learning Organization*. Doubleday.

Wheatley, M. (2006) *Leadership and the New Science: Discovering Order in a Chaotic World*. Berrett-Koehler Publishers.

CONCLUSION

This is The Six 'I's of Innovation®. A circular, not linear, map. Participating in or leading innovation is a journey; it has dead ends, long stretches of barren road and often just a vague sense of where to take the next step. It requires a complex raft of skills, mindsets and capabilities to make it happen, plus good timing and large doses of serendipity, coincidence and luck.

We need to develop *curiosity* so we can *identify* needs.

We need to develop *creativity* so we can *ignite* new ideas.

We need to develop *critical* thinking so we can *investigate* what we want to create.

We need to develop *courage* to *invest* in decisions when we do not know what the outcome may be.

We need to develop *commitment* to see things through, to *implement* and stand up in the face of disappointment.

We need to develop the ability to be *clever*, to *improve* and rapidly learn from failure.

It is The Six 'I's®, working together in alignment and Purpose, that enables innovation to happen.

There is no such thing as one set of skills required to innovate. There are multiple skills needed.

There is no such thing as a culture of innovation. There are multiple cultures that are needed to make innovation flourish.

There is no such thing as one innovative mindset. There are multiple mindsets we need to cultivate in ourselves and others.

The important thing is to know what to deploy and when.

Harnessing diversity is the lifeblood of innovation.

So why, if it is so difficult, should we step out of our comfort zones and actively participate in or even be leaders of innovation?

If our current thinking is not going to help us solve the problems and challenges we currently face, then today is the day to start to challenge your own way of thinking.

When you finish this book, take out a piece of paper and draw three circles.

In one, write all the things that you think you are good at – your skills, your experiences, your talents.

In another, write your interests, your passions and what you most desire to see in the world. In the last circle, write the areas that you consider most significant and ready for innovation.

Is it science, education, religion and spirituality or politics, business, the arts or technology, health or media and entertainment, to name a few?

All of these are in constant flux and change; all of them need new thinking and people courageous enough to lead them into an unknown future.

Sense which one draws you in the most.

Within the intersection of these three circles lies your *Purpose*.

This is your sweet spot.

This is the place to start.

Yes, you can innovate.

WHAT NEXT?

It is my hope that this book has inspired you to be a serial innovator on the small and the big things in your life and work. The Six 'I's® can be reapplied over and over again and, each time, you will learn something new about yourself, your colleagues and the nature of innovation. Innovation is not just a process or an outcome, it is a daily practice and, like developing any new skill, it takes time and effort.

To help you do this, please visit our website www.6-i-innovation.com to find out new developments that we have created to help support your innovation efforts.

As well as practical tools, assessments and example case studies of organisations using The Six 'I's®, we are constantly developing supporting services to help individuals and organisations innovate. These include Six 'I's® training, talks, seminars, workshops, products, apps, tool kits and end-to-end innovation management software programs.

Also, if you would like either individual or team support in applying The Six 'I's® to your innovation challenges, please get in touch to find out more about our coaching and workshop facilitation services.

We look forward to hearing how you are getting on and continuing to support you in your innovation journey!

INDEX